Family Bible

sightline books

The Iowa Series in Literary Nonfiction

Patricia Hampl & Carl H. Klaus, series editors

Melissa J. Delbridge
Family Bible

University of Iowa Press, Iowa City

University of Iowa Press, Iowa City 52242
Copyright © 2008 by Melissa J. Delbridge
www.uiowapress.org
Printed in the United States of America
Text design by Richard Hendel

The University of Iowa Press is a member of
Green Press Initiative and is committed to
preserving natural resources.
Printed on acid-free paper

Library of Congress
Cataloging-in-Publication Data
Delbridge, Melissa J., 1952–
Family Bible / by Melissa J. Delbridge.
p.   cm.—(Sightline books: the Iowa series
in literary nonfiction)
ISBN: 978-1-58729-874-5 (pbk)
1. Delbridge, Melissa J., 1952 – .   2. Tuscaloosa
(Ala.)—Biography.   I. Title.
CT275.D34157A3 2008   2007043968
976.1'84063092—dc22
[B]

FOR CHARLES, FOR SUSAN, AND FOR CADY ERICKSON.

EACH GAVE ME SO MANY GIFTS.

*There's things going on in this man's world that are likely
to disturb any real genteel or refined type persons.*
—GEORGE C. WALLACE

*When you are as old as I, young man, you will know that there
is only one thing in the world worth living for, and that is sin.*
—LADY SPERANZA WILDE

Trust everybody, but cut the cards.
—FINLEY PETER DUNNE

Contents

Acknowledgments

I had great help with this project. Believe me. I offer my deepest grati-tude to Angela Williams, for her faith and revision; to Glenn Gossett, Bill Erwin, Peggy Dean Glenn, Anne LeBaron, and Rick Turner, my Alabama compatriots; to Joan Garrabrant, Faith Hobson, Ron Layne, and Rette Maddox (true teachers, every damn one of them!); to the John Hope Franklin Center, Weymouth Center, and the Durham Arts Council for sanctuary and support; to Joe, Holly, Carl, and all the other wizards at University of Iowa Press; to my patient colleagues in Duke University Libraries; to Nancy Tilly, Carol Henderson, Ma-ria Hitt, Kristen Rademacher, and Susie Wilde, my friends and fellow writers; and to all members of my loved and long-suffering extended family—even the ones who were put on this earth to make me crazy.

I also thank the editors of the following magazines in which chapters in this book previously appeared, some in slightly different forms:

The introduction, "Hurricane Creek," "Baptism," and "Mimosa Park" appeared in *Southern Humanities Review,* volume 39, number 2 (Spring 2005).

"Gun and Bait" appeared as "West Greene and River Bend: Gun and Bait" in the *Antioch Review,* volume 64, number 4 (Fall 2006).

"Girls Turned In" appeared in *Third Coast,* issue 24 (Spring 2007).

As for my pals Richenal Ansano, Danna Bower, Lisa Creed, Dale Edgerton, David Ferriero, Steve and Wendy Hensen, Lynn Holdzkom, Joann Kleinneiur, Tania Rochelle, Ann Pancake, Michelle Robertson, Stephanie Sutherland, and Alison Wellsfry—what the hell would I do without you? You did me the honor of believing before I did.

Prologue

y relatives don't take travel lightly. Hell, a few of them pray before making a long-distance call. The morning I left Tuscaloosa, Alabama, for good in 1980, I stopped in for a farewell breakfast with my grandmother. After we ate, Grandma and my two maiden aunts, their hair still sleep-plaited down their backs, waved and called love and warnings from the front porch. "Now Melissa, don't you pick up any hitchhikers," Grandma said, snuggling herself up tighter in her housecoat. "You heard about that girl down near Coaling picked up a baldheaded colored man and got herself raped. We'll all be praying for you."

"No, Grandma. Don't you worry about me. I'd never pick up a hitchhiker."

Aunt Mike offered, "And honey, you might think this sounds crazy, but I read where if a man tries to rape you, you just get down and crawl up under your car. Can't nobody rape you under your car."

I nodded. "I'll keep that in mind, Aunt Mike."

Aunt Grace thought this over for a minute, then added, "Nope. Can't nobody rape you there. Might *shoot* you under your car, though."

The ages of these three women totaled two hundred years that day. Aunt Mike had lived in Alabama all her life except for a short time when she worked for the Western Union in Rome, Georgia. My grandmother only left once to honeymoon in Little Rock in 1923. And if Aunt Grace ever crossed the state line, I never heard tell of it.

I won't lie to you. My home state has been a simmering stew of religion, race, sex, and corruption ever since James Monroe signed the Alabama Enabling Act in 1819. Read Johnson Jones Hooper's Simon

Suggs tales if you don't believe me. And you can't make stew without water. The Black Warrior River and its tributaries gave the citizens of Tuscaloosa plenty, not that we were ever known to drink that much of it. Most of us, especially the Episcopalians, tend not to like the taste, preferring something fizzy or with a little more kick to it. We've always liked to swim in it, however, and fish in it. We sin and repent in it. We sweat it and pray for it to fall. And we even bathe in it when we have to.

Swimming and sex seemed a lot alike to me when I was growing up on the Black Warrior River in Tuscaloosa. You took off most of your clothes to do them and you only did them with people who were the same color as you. As your daddy got richer, you got to do them both in fancier places. Country club pools instead of public ones where you paid a quarter. Rooms at the Stafford Hotel (or at least back seats with leather upholstery) instead of creek banks somewhere out in the country or lying on your boyfriend's work shirt out in the woods or on top of an Indian mound, trying to swat the mosquitoes off his back and your own legs. Both sex and swimming could involve liquid, heat, inflatable protection devices, and the occasional unguent. And bad things, real bad things, could happen if you did not follow the rules. My family was big on talking about rules, but keeping them has never been our strong suit, especially in the sex department.

My mother once told me she met my father the year she made an emergency landing in a cornfield (although sometimes she calls it a pea patch), flying lessons being the rage among young women in the years just after Amelia's flight. They married fast and had my brother a year later. By the time I started school, my parents had built a little house in the shadow of the Old House—my father's mother's house. I grew up in a county where my grandmother's ancestors snagged land when Alabama first became a state. They started building and just never figured out when to stop. Until I was eleven, I had a room in their house and a room in ours. I would fall asleep at night wherever I was when my head started bobbing. At my parents' house on nights when she worked late Connie Lee Touchet sang me to sleep with her mournful songs about laying down burdens and wading in water and carrying weary loads.

I don't mean to sound *Gone-with-the-Wind*-ish. Most of my relatives would have found a better fit on the pages of Erskine Caldwell.

Maybe Faulkner if he was wrestling with a bad hangover. My grandmother and her daughters were each over six feet tall. They lived in the five rooms of the house you could heat to tolerable in January, and prayed nightly that the morning did not find them all crawling out from under a heap of termite-infested lumber.

Still, when I stayed over in the high bed at their house, my grandmother held me in her arms. My aunt Margaret (Mike to me) read Grimm or Andersen tales to me (my favorites being the ones with crafty trolls, kindly woodcutters, brothers changed to swans, and brave girls who wove blankets of nettles or told the truth to save themselves), and my aunt Grace brushed my waist-length hair until I dozed, watched over by three benevolent giantesses. I know that it is because of the women of my childhood that I have no fear of flying or work; that I believe in magic; that I sleep easily, deeply, and soundly at night; and that I always feel safe and protected in the world in spite of all that came later.

Four generations of my family lived within walking distance of the Old House, six if you counted the Touchets. I did count them, since they had put up with us for over a hundred years—at first, tangled up with us against their will, then by economic necessity or lack of other options, and finally from familiarity and perhaps some love. Sometimes I suspect they may have stayed out of curiosity to see what sort of foolishness my family would commit next. They had plowed, harvested, and cooked our food for decades, but never once swam with us or sat down to eat with us when my parents were home.

To say walking distance may be a stretch. It was only walking distance if I cut through the box factory lot by the woods and crossed the railroad track, which I was not allowed to do without my big brother because of hobos. This seemed stupid to me, as I had eaten countless hunks of pie with them on my grandmother's stoop. Feeding hobos was, according to Grandma, the best way to keep them from hightailing it down the tracks with a lineful of your laundry. One did try to get me to go down into the woods one evening when I was seven. I politely declined the invitation because I had written a kick-ass report about Alabama's four Indian tribes (CHOC-taw! CHICK-a-saw! CHER-o-kee! CREEK!! I'd chant them jumping rope). I was scheduled to read it first thing in the morning. I've always loved an audience and did not want to be late for school. I knew not to tell anyone about his invitation, that he'd get in trouble and after all, he hadn't done me any harm.

I had learned to do many useful things by the time I was seven. I knew not to swim without a buddy or ask for a hit on a seventeen-point hand in a game of black jack. I could shoot a deer and knew how to field dress it if there was someone to help me with the heavy parts. I could sing like an angel, make a devil's food cake, and produce embroidery so fine that the back was as pretty as the front, all the loose threads tucked and trimmed.

I love Tuscaloosa. I also believe it sprung up from the riverbanks for the solitary purpose of making me crazy. If I could give you a high-minded reason why I left Alabama after twenty-eight years, I would, but I'd be lying. I came to North Carolina to visit a friend from high school and just stayed on. Every time I go back, I fall in love with it again. Especially the language. People there give a damn about everything and they like talking about it.

Neva Whitman from the Methodist church and her mother-in-law bring a pan of Mexican cornbread to my grandma's house while I'm visiting. "Oh, honey," she says, eyes glistening with memory. "You look so much like your daddy. I'll never forget how he made the rounds totin' that bottle of Wild Turkey every Christmas morning." She shakes her head slowly.

"Thank you," I reply, wishing I had a slug about then. "I'll take that as a compliment."

"And I sure meant it as one. Your daddy was a pretty man. A pretty man inside and out."

Old Mrs. Whitman blows her nose and nudges her. "Well, Neva, she's pretty, too. Ain't she pretty? Got those pretty little feet. Just you look."

The three of us stare at my feet. My grandmother puts on her glasses so she can stare too and hobbles over with her walker. My feet don't look bad, thanks to the saleslady in the pharmacy. She helped me select a bottle of nail polish with as much enthusiasm and concern as if I had been picking out my wedding gown.

The words can make abrupt shifts from precious to obscene in the span of a sentence or two. I eat my lunch in a restaurant where I sometimes had Sunday dinner as a child. Many of the other diners look familiar, and I keep trying to find my classmates under what the years have added to them. An old man with elastic-waist pants speaks to a child at the next table.

"Purty little girl, what's your name?"

She answers with glee. "What's my name? Puddin' Tane. Ask me again and I'll tell you the same."

The old man laughs with her at the old ditty, smiles through the rest of his meal.

I hear a man in the booth in front of me ask his friend, "What kind of a woman would name a baby Poontang?"

"Whore like that one," his friend replied, tilting his chin to indicate the child's mother. "Lemme tell you a story about her . . ."

Aunt Mike's the last of the old ones. I take her fried catfish for dinner, and we eat with a lapful of paper towels on the front porch. She tells me the most recent neighborhood scandals as the players drive past. "There goes that new electrolysist. I guess that's what you call her. She went and married her an Indian. Least she says he's from India. Don't look much like any Indian I ever saw. Has those old thick fingernails?" She wrinkles her nose and flicks her nails significantly before changing the subject to the mailman's son. "Got himself fired from a good job at the waterworks several years back for pulling a Coke bottle on his boss. One of those pint-sized return-for-deposit ones. Busted the neck off first, I reckon. I hate to talk bad about him, though. They's two sides to every story."

Aunt Mike always wants to give me something when I leave her. She hands me a faded orange umbrella made of fabric passable in a flowery old-fashioned way. "It won't work no more, but I thought you might like to have it. It used to belong to your Aunt Grace." I try to open it and the spines splay like tiddlywinks. We touch them as if we held splinters of the true cross. "You mind nothing happens to it. And you be careful walking down that drive. You're back in the land of chiggers and copperheads now." Nobody else writes to me or talks to me the way she does anymore.

I drive over the viaduct so slowly that the car behind me swerves and screeches past me. Seeing the short wall of the walkway conjures the texture of the concrete on my seven-year-old palm. We crossed this bridge every morning on the way to school, Dolphus Barton yelling in a nasty singsong at the black children walking on the other side, "Two! Four! Six! Eight! We don't want to integrate!" The day finally came when one hollered back, a tall boy in high-top sneakers. "Eight! Six! Four! Two! I'll be going to school with you!" Got Dolphus good and we all laughed together till he snatched up a handful of rocks and everybody on both sides of the viaduct had the good sense to run.

If you've never spent time in Alabama, the strongest image you have of it probably came from the six o'clock news—police dogs barking and fire hoses spewing and Birmingham mayor Bull Connor barking and spewing about the necessity of keeping the races separate. Most of the stories in this book represent my attempt to record something new about the people who lived there, to let you see and hear them before they're dead, forgotten, or blended to oblivion. Like a family Bible, the book contains records of the events of generations, stories illustrating the codes by which my people lived. I'll tell them faithfully as I can and try to do it without condemnation or apology.

Memory never pours out nice and linear. Memory sidewinds, trickles out willy-nilly. Two people may hold the same recollection of a story, an event, and each may hold that memory dear, but when they draw them from the back of their consciousness, you can lay money on them dressing the players differently. Plots spindle and fold. That old gal who came dancing in yesterday may drag her feet by next October.

Writers have compared memories to ghosts, but most of mine don't so much haunt as they do nag, flitting around like a swarm of gnats too tiny for their appetites, stinging whatever part of me I forgot to cover. Swat as I may, they keep on coming.

A few other memories come slinking up, cowering and hesitant like some tail-tucked stray dog. I can shoo at him all I want. Put up fences and he'll dig right under. Hit him with a thrown rock and he'll scurry out of range but not sight, then skulk back up low-bellied, sideways, and shamed. The whole family may hate it, but he's ours for keeps now. Writing this book has been like coaxing that dog up onto the porch. Shoot, I can't even remember life before I called him home.

Family Bible

Hurricane Creek

n July of 1959, Coy Cullens's boxer mix Rufus jumped the fence and tore a big piece out of my brother's Little League pants and a smaller chunk out of his calf. Billy wrecked his bike and couldn't finish his paper route. Coy's wife felt so bad about it that she called her husband at the foundry, told him to get his ass home and true the bent tire. She came rolling the bike up the hill to our houses in her pedal pushers, a new pair of pants folded in the basket, the right color but the wrong size, to thank my daddy for shooting that damned dog. It was a good thing the tire got fixed, because Rufus did turn up rabid and Billy had to ride his bike to Druid City Hospital several times to get shots in his stomach so that Momma would not have to take off work. Billy said they didn't even hurt. Coy was sorry as he could be. To him it just didn't seem like a whole year had passed since Rufus got his shot, but he reckoned it must have been.

I tell you this now so you know right off that we were not, to say the least, over-protected children. We were loved with an amused distraction by parents both exasperated and hypnotized by one another's presence. Billy'd let the screen door slam behind him, his cheeks flushed after his shot, and Momma, just in from the lumber company, would embrace him, call him her brave and handsome little man, then her sentence would trail. The light in her eyes would shift when my father walked in, unbuttoning his shirt in the living room. We were adored when they remembered. My brother and I played Scrabble at night in the living room, Shell asleep on the rug beside us, and I would look up between turns and catch my mother looking at us puzzled, as if someone had left us on the doorstep, rung the bell, and run. When we asked her to play, she'd moan, "Honey, Mother's just too damn tired."

Family outings were not frequent events. Midautumn, Daddy might load us into his Harvester Scout and take us out in the woods near Samantha to pick the muscadines my grandfather made into syrupy wine. The day after Thanksgiving we'd all go to Burton and Loring jewelry store in downtown Tuscaloosa to let Momma pick out her Christmas present. She did it herself, insisting that Daddy's taste was all in his mouth. Every other spring we'd go down to Walker's Buick and pick out Momma a new red car. And once in a blue moon, Daddy'd take the day off and we'd all drive out to Hurricane Creek.

My mother drove with the window rolled down, ten miles over the speed limit, her elbow resting on the sill hard enough to leave a mark on her inner forearm. She invented road rage before 1960. Kept her red lips set tight and her eyes on the prowl for idiot drivers. "Did you see that idiot driver?" she'd ask, and I'd nod. My mouth would have been gaping if I had not remembered to keep it closed. Momma hated a mouth-breather. "Buddy," she'd mutter, "if you can't drive that wreck, you'd better damn park it!"

I never actually saw the idiot driver because I couldn't look without taking my eyes off her with those legs in her black two-piece. I squirmed between my parents on the hot plastic upholstery in my oldest bathing suit, a bright red one with the leg elastic half-blown and a field of picks on the butt from where I'd sat on the concrete without a towel. Billy and Michelle poked at each other in the back seat. I got the front by virtue of carsickness.

Momma'd take the turn at the Jungle Club too fast by a long shot, and we'd hit the bump, craning our necks to make sure we'd tied the trunk tight enough to keep the patched black inner tubes from flying out across the old Birmingham Highway. We were outside the city limits now.

We probably would have gone swimming more often if Daddy hadn't made more money working 11-to-7 than he did working 7-to-3 or 3-to-11. He was foreman at the paper mill, the boss of many of my friends' fathers, although I'd get slapped for mentioning it. He slept during the day when he was working third shift, and we grew up to his rhythm, knowing by the time we were four when to play quietly. Him going with us to swim gave the excursion a charge.

Momma swung in at the Jiffy Mart to buy him a six-pack. We waited in the car's closeness, me kneeling on the seat to stare at the kudzu-festooned Jungle Club across the two-lane highway. A ply-wood palm tree, its paint faded and its trunk bowed at the middle, leaned against the cinder-block building. A push broom propped the front door open but inside I could see only darkness. A black man with a name too small to read on his pocket unloaded boxes from the Pabst Blue Ribbon truck he'd parked between a mud hole and a pile of half-melted roofing tabs someone had meant to spread. When my father came back out to the car with a sack under his arm and got situated beside me, I asked him, "Daddy, what do people do in the Jungle Club?"

My mother answered for him in her Liz-Taylor-doing-Tennessee-Williams voice, moving her lips in an exaggerated manner and speaking through clenched teeth. "Oh, they just sit around drinking and telling lies and slipping their hands up their buddies' wives' skirts. And darling, your daddy's just about the best person in Tuscaloosa County you could ask that particular question."

Everybody said my father looked like Kirk Douglas when he smiled. He winked at me, breaking open a beer with the church key he kept in the glove compartment. He passed me the first sip and when he took the frosted can back, he brushed it along my mother's thigh like it was an accident, only real slow. She tossed her brunette waves back over her shoulder and smiled at her reflection in the rearview.

I watched my parents play variations of this scene a thousand times before they finally divided the furniture in 1964. It was both sorrowful and exciting to see—my mother simmering, simmering, then striking out sharp when that one more thing happened. When her high heel snapped off after eight hours doing payroll at the lumber company and him not home yet. When I fell out of the chestnut tree playing Pollyanna and my right ankle puffed up faster than a nickel balloon. Sometimes she'd shriek, sometimes curse through grinding teeth when the Scout finally pulled in. And he would pull her to him again and again, all slow smirking charm, reaching for her until she acquiesced. Accusations fizzled, never answered.

I closed my eyes because if you did you would notice how the sounds changed three times on the way to Hurricane Creek. When we turned off the highway, the roars of the eighteen-wheelers whizzing past our open windows gave way to the stickiness of the hot county blacktop sucking at whitewall. One sharp right, which Momma always nearly missed, and we listened for a few miles to the crunch and pop of gravel under Buick. Then we'd turn onto a jagged red dirt road that slowed even my mother down. She'd let the car roll easy, coasting the downhill curves, braking once in a while to maneuver the deeper ruts. Grasshoppers buzzed and whirred in the quiet. We could hear any sound our family made echoing back at us off the water in the deep cool ravine below.

Billy in his cutoffs was first out the door. He'd untie the trunk and bounce out the biggest inner tube and roll it ahead of him, yelping down the steep gully. I'd grab the next best and fall in behind, dancing all the way the way I danced everywhere until I turned twelve. Fine dried silt the texture of chocolate cake mix powdered my chipped orange toenail polish and my feet would pad, pad, soft down the slope to the sand and river rock shore, Shell whining behind for us to wait up while Momma attached her lime green water wings.

Momma came down slowly, surefooted but watching her step the same, carrying Shell. Daddy lumbered down last, laden with a sack of bologna sandwiches, a gallon jar of grape Kool-Aid, and Hydrox cookies, and a quilt made out of my old sunsuits, and his six-pack, now down to five.

Once Shell had been plopped down in the shallows, she knew to stay put. She'd paddle around, speckled by the sun filtering down through the branches, popping smooth pebbles into her mouth and spitting them out, laughing at their little splashes.

Hurricane Creek cut through a viny and rock-studded valley. Where we swam, it poured over a two-foot waterfall into the deep place where Shell and I were not allowed to go. Billy could, since he had passed his Minnow test, and he rushed down there to try out his new snorkel and frogman flippers, even though the creek wasn't really wide enough and his rabies-shot-sore belly would scrape sand after two or three kicks.

Once my parents spread the quilt that had seen better days, Momma took out her Coppertone and began the languorous anointing of her long legs. She passed the bottle to my father, now done with his second beer and contemplating the third, and turned her back to him, wordless, lowering her straps. Soon we were free from their surveillance.

I tiptoed out to where the brown creek water came up to my chin, feeling it so much colder below my knees, careful not to step into a hole and plunge over my head. I pushed my inner tube before me as I crossed. I had not even started my Tadpole class yet and could not swim a lick. I'd been age-eligible for two years, but nobody could take me to Queen City Pool since Connie Lee couldn't drive and Momma was working part-time. They had told me I could start at Minnow level come next summer if Daddy got promoted.

When I reached the other side, I saw a boy standing still at the top of the bank of the ravine, watching us. He wore cutoffs like Billy's, only the legs were hemmed instead of frayed. Way on up the hill, hanging onto a rope someone had knotted to a high branch, he rared back to swing out over the creek.

The little girl was smaller, perhaps my age. She stood so quiet that I did not see her until I came close. She wore only a pair of dingy white cotton panties, thin as a tissue. Her hair was braided in places and secured with red strings, and her nipples looked like tiny black clusters of tight French knots on her chest. We both flinched our shoulders when her brother splashed down into the water even further than Billy could reach with his best running start. I caught the rope when it swung back our way and passed it to her.

Instead of reaching for it, she dropped her face and clasped her hands behind her back as if to hold them back from snatching the rope from my hands. "Here, go ahead. Y'all were here first," I insisted, for I had not yet learned that my best manners were not meant to be used with everybody.

The girl mouthed thank you without a sound coming out, took the rope, and climbed the hill high as her brother had. A few running steps and she jumped, hoisting her body up so that she swung with her elbows bent, the rope held to her chest like Tarzan. Distinct muscles swelled all over her little brown arms and when she let go, she slid into the deep water with her toes pointed, barely splashing at all. Watching her from the hill, I felt a pull in my chest firm as a tugged drawstring. For the first time, I was physically aware of the beauty of another human creature.

I let the rope swing back past me, ashamed to let her see the way I could only dangle limp as a puppet. I jumped into my inner tube from a mossy rock, and spun it around her way just in time to see her shoulder and leg disappearing into the brush down a path, the way you might think you'd seen a deer go. Her brother had vanished as well. She did not look back or wave goodbye to me.

"Who were those kids?" I asked my father while I sprinkled crunched-up potato chips on my sandwich. Billy stuck out his tongue to disgust me with the black paste of a chewed-up Hydrox. Daddy opened one eye. "Probably Jesse's kids. They live somewhere back up in there. Him or Luther's one." Momma rolled over onto her stomach and sighed. "Y'all go play now."

I jumped off the rock several more times, toes pointed, trying not to splash. The rope saw no more action that day. It just was not fun anymore. While my parents slept away the afternoon, wrapped around each other, I circled round and round in the tube, pretty much waiting to go home, avoiding the water bugs skittering over the places behind the rocks where the water stilled. I stayed away from those pockets scummed with yellow, with slimed branches and snake spit.

Late that afternoon, the sun ducked behind clouds and the air cooled fast. Shell was sleeping on the quilt beside my parents. The water seemed to turn darker, as if large shapes moved beneath, and the wind crimped the surface. I got out and sat on the shore, picking at my pruned fingertips. We had run those children off and I knew it. I wasn't even sure how, but I did know I felt ashamed of myself. The little girl could walk there anytime she wanted to, could swim without permission. It was her place. Her father had probably hung the rope swing. She belonged there, and I, in my stupid red ruffled raggedy-assed bathing suit, did not.

To this day, if I am feeling guilty about something I have done or something I have neglected, this is the place where my dreams will take me. To a slow creek through a ravine where the shade plants are too large, greener than any ferns, extinct everywhere else on earth. It is coming on evening and I am chilled to notice the dark shapes moving ponderously beneath the surface of the deep brown water. I cannot see them clearly enough to know what they are, and I am too afraid of them to wade in closer.

Mimosa Park

y parents were at war in 1964, much as they had been all my life, but this time without the hot truces which had always kept them coming back swinging for the next round. Rumors made the rounds of neighbors and hunting cronies—rumors about him and the Tri-Delt or the scoutmaster's wife. Momma heard them and doors got slammed and supper got burned and we all forgot to feed the dog. Billy and Shell and I turned up the volume so we could hear "The Three Stooges" over their threats and accusations.

We weren't particularly upset by their misbehavior, as I recall, having grown up with my mother pretty much on a steady rolling boil. They'd always fought over everything from my ballet lessons (she insisted) to his hunting trips (a week long at River Bend and no phone and what if something happened to one of the kids?). Their seething and forgiving was the cadence of our lives. More than once I hurried home from school for my ballet lesson, slipped out of my jumper and into my leotard and slippers, and ran outside to help Daddy butcher a ten- or twelve-point buck hanging upside down, throat slit, from my swing set. Daddy chopped off the lower half of the front hoof and showed me which tendon to pull to make the hoof contract. Momma hollered out the window for me to get in the goddamned car before I got rabies, ticks, and hookworms, and soon I'd be at Inge's perfecting my arabesque to Tchaikowsky, red-palmed and sporting a bloody hoof print on my pink tights.

Things got real bad between them the summer Queen City Pool closed down, before I could learn to swim properly. When the government told us we had to integrate it, the white people fought for a while, then they threw up their hands and they all quit going. Some well-meaning liberals did their level best to keep it open for a couple of years for the children who had always watched from up by the railroad track at the top of the hill, but townspeople got worried about there being trouble down there with all of that congregating going on, and soon it closed on down. The aquamarine pool with its pink shell fountain, designed by a student of Frank Lloyd Wright, gathered leaves and broken bottles, cracked its glaze, and lay empty for years. When I was in college, a fashion photographer took artsy pictures of me standing on the diving board in a fur coat and high-heeled shoes—an ad for Doris Hill's swanky downtown dress shop. It ran full page in the *Tuscaloosa News* the Sunday before the Alabama-Auburn game. My family was proud of me. Thanks to Mike Dubose's last-minute recovery of an Auburn fumble, the score was 17 for the Tide, 13 for the animal husbands. After my father died in 1996, I found a yellowed copy of the ad folded in his wallet and thought he'd kept it for the football coverage till I saw myself on the other side.

When I told her I was writing about places where we swam, my sister Shell recalled the diving platform at Mimosa Park, her standing at the top of it in her red Jantzen swimsuit with a tiny lady diver above the thigh elastic. She remembers that summer much better than I, fills me in on the details. On a trip home, she found an old postcard of the pool in its heyday in Boyd's antique shop.

Seeing the photograph of the pool at Mimosa Park Country Club disappointed me. In the picture, all I saw was a middle-sized pool by a low-roofed structure, surrounded by rough gray concrete and a gaggle of splashing flat-topped towheaded boys. A huge gray square hole nothing like the pink-and-turquoise splendor of Queen City. What I could remember were carnival rides; a fountain bubbling up at the entrance like a promise of joy to come; tall curlicued wrought-iron gates flung wide open. Driving in, members heard summer music, flirtatious laughter, and the shrieking from a menagerie comprised of seven apes and a lonesome wildcat. Pretty women in two-piece suits waved carefree from the lake as they water-skied past the stands. The diving platform was said to be the tallest in the state.

Mimosa Park Country Club wasn't a country club. Not really. Not the kind where rich people played tennis and drank two too many martinis. By calling it that, though, by having a charter and a membership fee rather than an admission fee, the owners made it legal for themselves to get to choose what color people came through the gates and what color could only work there or watch from the hillside.

To be honest, I was surprised that my mother joined, not that she or anyone else I knew in my youth had any problem with the segregation of recreational venues. She was just tight with money—selective about which luxuries she'd spring for. My ballet lessons from the German instructor rather than the less expensive Neva Jean's School of Dance, yes. Real leather shoes for her children, from the best store in town, yes. A country club? Silly snobs. Not on your life.

But in my first two-piece suit, a black-and-white one with piping on the seams, I did not question or second-guess our good fortune. Several of the cool girls from my school were members, too, and I hoped that we would become friends over the summer, easing the transition into the sixth grade. Betsy Cotrell swam there. I usually was not encouraged to socialize with Betsy because of what happened to her big sister Emily, a scandal all over the county (and him a married man) in spite of the story her family spread about her studying in France. Not the most plausible nine-month alibi they could have invented, given how even Emily Cotrell's English barely passed muster. Then again, the Cotrells had never exactly been celebrated for their creativity.

It was evident that rules were made to be broken at Mimosa Park. Betsy and I paddled and basked and twitched our girlish behinds in their unsuitable suits around the pool all summer, and my mother, engrossed in long conversations with our neighbor, paid us no mind.

Strange though it seemed, another family from Pine Park Circle had joined Mimosa Park. The Linneys, who lived way on down the road in something more than a trailer but not quite a house and who did not have a pot to pee in, had joined around the same time we did. Gus Linney was the chubby-faced dunce of the remedial reading group in my sister's class. He was cursed with a tendency to blubber like a baby with snot running down whenever teased, although you'd have thought he'd have gotten used to it, often as it happened. His mother Nita, a Cuban woman from Miami, spoke English worse than any Cotrell yet born and never once came to the pool. My father grumbled about paying the membership fee every month and never showed his handsome face there either.

Gus's father, Billy Linney, was handsome too, but in an open-faced and goofy way too young for his age. He gave me and my girlfriends quarters to buy Cokes and never seemed to tire of Marco Polo. He watched me more closely than my own father did, and always made certain that my sunscreen was smoothly applied to my back. Didn't I look like a picture in my new two-piece, my mother asked him, and when we were alone, he agreed, whispering to me.

I had my concerns about having to hang out with Gus, and the possible effect this association could have on my budding friendship with Betsy, but I saw no way around it. I knew I could not ignore a boy who, by the second week in July, was sharing a bucket of fried chicken with us every Thursday. Sometimes Gus and Billy Linney would bring Cindy, the two-year-old who showed no interest in anything and had not a hair on her oddly shaped head, and stick her in the baby pool. Early August I heard a fat lady shriek and ran over to pull Cindy out sputtering when I saw her floating face down. My mother received glares of disapproval from the baby pool mothers, which confused me until I realized they thought Cindy belonged to her. For the rest of the summer I was paid the first money I ever earned—two dollars a day—to watch her.

Come September and I'm off to school with the largest papery-shelled specimen from my seven-year-locust collection stuck on purpose to my red sweater and a handful of spider lilies for Miss Menning, my new teacher. Mimosa Park closed down for the summer and Nita Linney moved on down to Miami with her disadvantaged children in tow.

Shell and I shared a yellow bedroom (my favorite color because she was too little to have one when we built the house) with long lace curtains from the time she was toilet-trained till all hell broke loose that fall and our lives changed forever in the middle of the night. Momma was the PTA Room Mother Chairman, as always ("I don't know how she does it, what with a full-time job and all!" marveled Jean Crewe, who later became either my daddy's third or fourth wife), and you had to walk sideways down our hall past all the cardboard boxes full of Halloween favors for the Alberta Elementary School Halloween Carnival. Connie Lee had shaken her head and shoved them all to one side to keep the floor furnace from setting us all on fire.

Deer season had started and Daddy had scrubbed his stubble on my cheek as I gave him his goodnight sugar, his rifle stock pressing into my tummy. He was off to River Bend, and I had been asleep almost five hours when Momma woke me up cussing. She had stubbed her foot on one of the Halloween boxes. Shell was whining when Momma shoved a cardboard box onto my bed.

"Sugar, get up and get dressed and pack your school clothes and don't you dare forget those new red shoes. River Bend, my ass! Nobody at the River Bend Hunting Club's seen hide nor hair of your daddy this week and I've had it up to here with his gallivanting around! We'll come back for your play-pretties next week."

She made us pack in the dark so my grandmother in the big house next door wouldn't ask any of her damn nosy questions. Half-asleep, I surveyed my belongings. How could I choose? I took my toe shoes, my Louisa May Alcott books, a few changes of clothes, my locust-shell collection, and my transistor radio. Shell took Raggedy Ann and a mismatched pair of pajamas. Billy packed his Boy Scout handbook, Marty Robbins records, and black high-topped Keds.

Now this is the part I don't remember, but Shell does. She says Momma had just stuck the key in the ignition when I opened the car door and jumped out and ran back into the unlocked house, her hissing threats at me to get my butt back in the car. Shell tells me that when they found me inside, I was up on the yellow metal stepstool Momma had gotten with Green Stamps. I was crying on my tiptoes, struggling to pull the box of our baby pictures down from the top shelf of my mother's closet. Momma grabbed my elbow and started to yank me down and the Buster Brown shoebox slid and spilled. Black-and-white snapshots and colored 8×10s from my ballet recitals covered the hardwood, and I hit the stepstool, then the floor on my left knee, bloodied it, and started scrambling for the photographs.

I don't know what my mother did then. When I try to imagine the scene, I see her standing with her mouth open, like someone caught guilty of a lie and fishing for an explanation, holding the empty box to her chest. I scrambled to keep a few of our photographs and to grab my parakeet's cage on our way out the door. Here is the list of the pictures I kept:

My mother holding me on the way home from the hospital two days after my birth, me with a headful of ringlets, smiling and looking like a three-month-old.

Shell and me in one of our recitals, me in blue satin and a pinafore with three inches of taffeta petticoat showing, as Alice in Wonderland. Shell was a hula girl.

Me and Billy and my pretty little cousin Nan playing Old Maid.

Billy grinning gap-toothed with a stringer full of bream he caught
on the Black Warrior River.

All of us in Easter clothes, posing in front of the Harvester Scout.

My father, bare-chested and handsome, showing off a wildcat he
shot dead at River Bend. He kneels with his knees spread, gripping the carcass between his thighs by the scruff of her neck
so her teeth are bared as if she's alive and ready for a fight. Her
body, however, reveals the truth. It dangles limp, like she's just
plum worn out. There is a small crease across the upper right
corner of the picture where my mother tried to snatch it from
my hand, but I refused to let it go.

That night Momma moved us into a tiny rented house on a dead-
end street on the other side of town. The bushes had stickers instead
of gardenias. Momma said we'd go back one day to get my books, but
we never did. Over the past forty years I've replaced some of the ones
I remember best. The room I shared with my sister in the new house
was beige, and I started two months into the year at a new school
where the sixth-grade girls wore bras and watched "Gidget" movies.
I put my locust shells away in a cigar box, knowing the other girls
would think them babyish. It would be hard enough to start my new
life without them thinking I was country-come-to-town. I did not see
my grandmother and aunts again for nearly two years, as they did not
drive and it was too far for me to walk or ride my bike. We sure as
hell could not afford my ballet lessons or Connie Lee. And Momma's
family just shook their heads. They had known all along that something like this would happen, her marrying so young. Marrying a man
so far beneath her. A man she met one summer in some goddamned
Alabama cornfield.

Shot Rule

What woman alive knows why her mother is the way she is? Mine felt cheated her whole life and from what she's told me, I believe her. Cheat her long enough and any woman will turn bitter on you. Catch my mother in the right mood and she will list lost treasures that should have been hers. Her own mother left her husband before Momma started school, then married again. Once she had a new daughter and son, she packed my mother off to live with her grandmother. And eventually, Momma found a man guaranteed to deceive her again and again and married him in a heartbeat. All that wrongdoing took a steep toll over time.

When my grandmother died, she left everything to the children of her second marriage. This did not surprise my mother. By then she had come to expect betrayal. To this day she thinks she sees it coming down the road toward her when it's really not even in the neighborhood.

None of these familial wounds cut her as deeply, to hear her tell it, as what happened in a piano competition the year she turned ten. My mother started playing piano when she was five, and by the time she entered third grade, she played so well that her piano teacher, Mrs. Maxwell, helped her to fill in an entry form for a statewide contest, assuring my mother she had a good chance of winning the hundred-dollar prize—an unimaginable jackpot for a child in 1937. Wearing a pinafore her grandmother had made her, she tucked her hair behind her ears and stepped onstage.

She played Auguste Durand's *Valse, opus* 83—a difficult fluttering waltz, all presto and vivo and brillante, with three flats, some jumping to naturals here and there, and an occasional sharp thrown in just to make sure you paid close attention. The prize went to a curly-headed rich girl in a lacy dress. She played a much simpler tune, but bounced adorably in rhythm, frequently turning her face to dimple at the judges. Little darling.

Twenty-three years later, I was nine years old. Momma wheeled her red Buick into a densely potholed parking lot of the county clinic, grazing the curb and inventing a parking place—one that looked like it just might pass for legal—where she would not have to walk too far in her high heels. She hated those shoes, but my father and her boss at Jennings Lumber Company liked what they did for her legs, so she stabbed her feet into them every morning, swearing at Daddy if he was at home to whistle at her. And she kicked them off, land where they will, first thing in the evening when she got home, dog-cussing Mr. Jennings.

"Now just you remember we're coming here one time and one time only," she warned us, as if we'd beg to repeat the trip. Usually, we saw Dr. Folsom in an air-conditioned office where we sat in upholstered chairs reading *Highlights* magazine. By appointment only. "And you are never to mention this visit to anyone—and that means anyone, do you hear me? Especially not to your teachers and not to your Grandma Standridge."

I nodded. Since we left the house, my mother had complained about having to take an hour off from her job at the lumber company accounting office. "Dragging my children across town to this filthy place and waiting in line like some migrant field hand." She had tried and failed to make an appointment for our shots. "And don't you let me catch you sitting down in here. Every filthy urchin in Tuscaloosa County will be shedding impetigo over all available surfaces." She flipped the rearview mirror down and to the left and swiped at her mouth with a red lipstick worn flat on the tip. "If your father brought home his goddamned paycheck instead of gallivanting all over kingdom come flashing his wad at every honky-tonk and poker game and God-knows-where-else, you would not have to endure this humiliation!"

My mother was speaking more to herself than to us, the way she often did. I mouthed the words to help me remember. Gal-li-vant-ing. Mi-grant. Im-pe-ti-go. Thanks to my mother's perpetual vituperations and my dog-eared seventeen-year-old *Webster's Collegiate Dictionary,* I had both a vocabulary that left my teachers shaking their heads and a good shot at the county spelling bee that night.

"No way to rig a spelling bee," Momma said. "With words, you either spell them right or you spell them wrong and you do it right there in front of witnesses." She dropped her car keys into her bulging purse. "Not like some contests," she continued, "where the judges can just pick whoever winks at them or wears a pink dress. And your only competition's that asthmatic little Rhonda Jennings. Last time I saw her onstage she got so scared they had to stop the recital in the middle of 'My Heart Belongs to Daddy' to mop up the floor." The fact that Rhonda was her boss's daughter magnified Momma's satisfaction.

"How do you spell 'humiliation'?" I asked.

"Just read the sign over that goddamned door, honey," she muttered. I looked up. Tuscaloosa County Health Department. I noticed that one brunette strand from the wave over my mother's brow had fallen too low. I wanted to reach up, to smooth it back into place, but decided against it. I'd remember to look up the word myself. I would remember to not touch a thing in the clinic, to not sit down. I would not speak to anyone except my mother and the nurse. Above all, I would not cry when the nurse stuck me.

My brother and sister and I stood silent in our church clothes, our backs against the wall in the immunization clinic's waiting room. Not quite as bad as taking a number and waiting for someone to call it, but almost. Six metal chairs waited empty near an open window where we might have caught something like a breeze, but my mother forbade us to sit. "Rusty things," she muttered through her frozen public smile. "Pinch yourself in this godforsaken place and you'd probably die of lockjaw." So we stood, hands folded in front of us, breathing the odors of carbolic, rubbing alcohol, and floor-cleaning rosin. Every time the door opened, Momma glanced over to see if the new patient might recognize her, then turned away fast. G-O-D-F-O-R-S-A-K-E-N. I called up the letters in my mind.

Other children, dressed in jeans and overalls, squabbled over a pile of toys that had seen better days. I watched them playing in the center of the room. I wiggled a few fingers and lifted one corner of my mouth to acknowledge a greeting from Cheryl, a preacher's daughter I knew from my school. I helped her with her reading every day.

I did not learn to read early, but I had started school starving to do it and picked it up fast. "My girl could have read that standing on her head with one eye shut two years ago!" my mother had complained to Mrs. Cook at the last parent-teacher conference, flipping through the third-grade reader and slapping it down on the desk. While she disapproved of the delivery, my teacher concurred. The next day when I got up to sit in the circle with my reading group, she handed me a copy of *Little Women* and sent me back to my seat. We'd discuss it when I finished, she told me, then asked if I would mind tutoring some of the children who needed a little extra help.

I brought her a big handful of red spider lilies the next morning. Every day for the rest of the school year, I sounded out letters with my classmates. I took care to enunciate, since I'd lost my two front teeth in a playground accident five years earlier and the new ones were taking their time popping back through.

I had tried to jump out of a swing at Jaycee Park the way my brother Billy did. I watched him closely, because that was the way to learn, I knew. And I did learn, only I missed one of the subtle points of swing-jumping. I let go while the swing was heading backward instead of forward. I leapt out and caught myself, crouched on my hands and knees, laughing and proud for a second of victory before that heavy wooden swing soared back down and caught the back of my skull, catching a curl in a crack and yanking it out by the root. It slammed me facedown on hardpacked dirt. Knocked the wind right out and left me gasping and spitting blood, rage, and baby teeth. Nine years old now and still not a new incisor in sight. I felt the empty space with my tongue now and then, always hoping to catch something pushing through.

Cheryl got up from the waiting room floor and dropped the lopsided structure she had built out of Lincoln Logs. She scratched at a scab on her ankle and started toward me, but I glanced up at Momma, then furrowed my brow and shook my head. Cheryl plopped back down before my mother noticed.

My mother had taught us a rule for every act, from attending Sunday school to trying on new shoes. Guidelines for eating spaghetti and for getting shots. We knew not to play on escalators and how to coax noodles onto the fork with a spoon by the time we started school. She did not allow my hair to be braided because she loved the curls and hated the waves the plaiting caused. She taught posture by example. You could just look at her and know how to carry yourself. She held her shoulders back and stretched her neck to its full extension, walking with long confident strides even when I knew her feet felt like they were about to break in two.

And she saw visual reminders everywhere. She could not turn her head without laying eyes on a potential object lesson, and she delivered these at every opportunity. On the way to school, she would pull over in front of a neighbor's house and spit out her words with the motor still running. "Do you see that? Look how trashy that yard full of weeds looks! That sorry Oren Weaver never edged a flowerbed in his life. And I swear to God if a child of mine ever left their toys outside like that, it would be a cold day in hell before I bought her another one! I don't know how those poor people ever find a thing in that house."

I knew this to be gospel. I lay on my belly on the floor of the Weavers' train wreck of a living room almost every day after school while Momma kept books at the lumber company. After I helped Lizzie with her homework, we'd eat store-brand potato chips out of the bag and play scratched 45s on a portable record player with its tone arm weighted down by a taped-on dime. Pepsi caps took the place of checkers, and buttons stood in for the top hats and Scotties in Lizzie's Monopoly game. When we both reached for the magenta crayon, instead of waiting her turn while I used it, Lizzie'd snap it flat in two without thinking twice. Her games, her toys, her whole wonderful house were an unbelievable mess.

Momma took advantage of the noise in the lobby to remind us of the shot rule. "Now you listen to me. Melissa, pull up your socks. Cry while you wait and you'll look like an idiot. Cry when you get the shot and the nurse will think you're a sissy or some ill-begotten brat who's never been taught better. Cry on your way out and you'll scare these less fortunate children half to death, poor things, and they have to come here all the time. I have not raised crybabies, and I damned sure won't buy a crybaby an ice cream soda when we're done."

Billy, who never cried over shots, smirked at me. I smoothed the pleats of my skirt and raised my chin, determined. Ice cream from the soda fountain was an infrequent pleasure. I had blown it last time over a tetanus shot necessitated by a bicycle skid that had scraped off a good portion of my right cheek, and the time before that when strep throat landed me a hipful of penicillin that hurt so bad that I had just lain there sobbing, my vision of a sundae melting away in my mind.

Once I overheard my mother's friend Ora challenge the shot rule. "Oh, Margie," she chided. "That's too harsh. What does it hurt if they cry a little? They're just children."

My mother put down her coffee mug and stared, astonished, as if Ora had suggested that she sell us to the circus. "If you love your kids you draw those lines, Ora. Hard lines that won't budge. If you don't, they'll mire down, just mire right down and it's up to you to raise them up. What else do my kids have? Certainly not wealth. Don't all parents want better for their children? All parents except my damned husband."

Ora started trying to calm her, reaching for her hand across the table. "Now, Margie . . ."

"Oh, not George. Not George Delbridge. He seems to love the way he grew up. Only a dollop of homemade plum jam for a sweet and no shoes in the summer. School second to farm chores and hooky half the time. And look at him. What's he got to offer now?"

Ora smiled. "Charm, Margie. Your George has charm." She brought the percolator to the table and refilled Momma's cup. "Way more charm than the law should allow."

"Delbridge." The nurse called our name. Billy nodded and followed her down the hall. I took my little sister's hand and came behind, my mouth set in a line, heels clicking on the cracked linoleum. The door to the examination room swung shut behind us. I kept my breathing even and slow as I watched the nurse pierce the bottle top and draw up a serum thick as sorghum into the three syringes, then snap them down in a row onto sterile chrome trays.

No way around it. I knew the shot was a necessity, knew all about what it prevented. Grandma Delbridge and my maiden aunts cautioned me every time they saw me running in the Alabama heat. *Baby, get in out of that sun before you get too hot and catch polio. Come up here on the porch before you end up like that poor little Madison girl.* And I'd come to them, barefooted, forehead glowing with sweat beads, remembering how the Methodists would wheel Betsy Madison out every Thanksgiving and get her to sing "Bless This House." A beautiful voice, they said, and, one breath later, what a pity. My mother complained all the way home about the way they exploited that pathetic crippled child to fill up their offering plate.

E-x-p-l-o-i-t-e-d. I spelled to keep my mind away from the needles on the green mottled countertop, to focus on a jaybird hollering in the scrub oak outside. I did not want polio, but my heart felt like it was beating way too fast. I could see it pumping through my dress, feel it under my ears. The nurse pulled three cotton balls out of a glass cylinder and soaked the first in alcohol, then wiped Billy's arm and injected him. His eyelids fluttered a little, and he clenched his jaw and looked straight ahead, blinking fast until she withdrew the hypodermic and stuck a Band-Aid on his bicep. "It didn't even hurt. Shots never hurt me," he announced. My mother smiled at her only son.

The nurse turned to me. I struggled with the button on my left sleeve. Momma pushed Shell forward instead. "This that baby was so sick?" the nurse marveled. Everyone in Tuscaloosa had heard about Shell's battle with spinal meningitis four years earlier. Momma nodded and rolled down Shelly's sock to display the puckered scar on her ankle with reverence, like the child had sprung stigmata. "That's from all the transfusions. Wouldn't know it now, would you? Three months in pediatric intensive care. She's my miracle." Shelly dimpled, then laughed and reached for the nurse's nametag.

"Aren't you a chubby little monkey now?" teased the nurse, and Shell was swabbed and stuck before she had a chance to cry, and cooed when the nurse made a funny face and told her in a cartoon voice what a big girl she was.

My mother swept her miracle into her arms, not noticing that I had turned to her for help with the button. The nurse put down the syringe and assisted me.

"Usually we see Dr. Folsom over on Tenth Street East," Momma explained. "I'm sure you know him? He delivered all three, and I swear this baby's only alive because he stayed up all night long and prayed with her in his arms when all the other doctors gave up on her." I shuddered when the cold alcohol touched my skin.

During the months my mother had spent in the hospital with Shell, I had stayed with my father's mother in the Old House. Every night my aunts would scrub me with an orange cake of Lifebuoy soap till it chapped my skin, fearing that meningitis germs lurked in my pores. Ancient clocks would chime the hours and the echoes moved from room to room as if they were looking for something lost. The aunts dosed me daily with a prescription to keep me from getting what my sister had, but I cried so at the taste that they took to mixing the drug with honey and spreading it on a graham cracker, feeding it to me as a treat. They did not know I hated honey. I would thank them for the goody and skip outside to bury it or feed it to the dogs, all except for the night dose. That one I hid in a drawer at the base of the oldest grandfather clock and never did get caught.

Momma chattered on. "A miracle, an absolute miracle's what it was. We never go anywhere but Dr. Folsom's, but this was just so convenient for me today with all this PTA spelling hoopla tonight. I'd rather slam my thumb in the car door than go, but this one's gonna make her momma proud, aren't you, sweetheart?"

"Yes, ma'am." I made the mistake of looking at my blue veins through the skin of my skinny wrist as the nurse pushed the needle into my muscle. I rubbed my tongue rhythmically over the gap where my teeth were missing and spelled to myself. P-a-t-h-e-t-i-c. The bite of the needle grew brighter and brighter, then stopped just in time.

"There now, sugar. Not so bad, was it? Just a little bee sting." I smiled and turned to my mother as the nurse taped a round Band-Aid over the blood droplet. Before I could take a step, the nurse grabbed my chin and turned my face toward the harsh fluorescent light. "Good Lord! What on earth happened to this child's teeth?" she exclaimed, squinting.

I tried to turn away, but the nurse clamped her fingers around my face and lifted my upper lip with her thumb. She bent closer. I felt something in my chest drop the way it had when Pinkie Floyd had opened the door of the toilet stall while I was peeing, only now there was nothing to pull up or down to hide myself from the nurse's examination. Shame flooded up hot into my cheeks.

"Oh, it's nothing," Momma replied, pulling me away from the nurse's hold and heading for the door. "Just a playground accident a few years back. The dentist says they'll come in just fine pretty soon."

"Well, I'd sure have them looked at if she was mine." The nurse wrinkled her brow. "Nine's a little old for them to still be missing. Might be something broken off in there keeping them from coming in."

"Thank you so much for your concern," my mother muttered.

"It would make a huge difference in her looks, and it might save you a lot of money in braces if they come in all crooked." She handed me three suckers. "One for each, honey." I tried to keep the tears from coming. Failing, I shrugged my shoulder and turned my reddened face away from my mother.

But she had seen me cry. She snatched the lollipops and stuffed them into her purse on her way out the door. "That b-i-t-c-h must have more dollars than she does sense," she hissed, striding down the hall. "Like I have time and money to run to a goddamn dentist every time a child loses a baby tooth! And you in there squawling like a heathen! Honest to God, Melissa, I don't even know why I try."

As we rounded the corner in the long hall, Billy ran smack into Rachel Weaver, hard enough for her watch to leave an imprint on his cheek. "Excuse me, ma'am," he apologized, reaching for her elbow. "Are you all right?"

"Oh, honey, I'm just fine. And what a little gentleman! Why, Margie, I'm surprised to see you here. Weren't you just talking last week about how y'all always use Dr. Folsom?"

"Oh, good afternoon, Rachel. Yes, my Billy's always had the best manners." Momma answered lightly, patting her hair into place and stalking past. "I don't know where he got them," she called back. "Sure as hell wasn't from his daddy!" She left Mrs. Weaver smiling at the empty hall ahead of her, the question unanswered.

I grinned at Cheryl as we rushed out through the waiting room. I hoped we were far enough away that she could not see my swollen eyes. Cheryl had enough problems with phonics and did not need me scaring her witless.

My mother ripped into the red lollipop's cellophane with her teeth when we reached the car. She turned the key in the ignition and began singing a tango along with the radio temptress. "I know that I must have your kiss although it DOOOOOMS me, though it con-SYOOOOMS me . . ." I was relieved that my mother was singing. Maybe her mood would shift now. I sat in the back seat, staring at her shoes and considering the words. D-o-o-m. C-o-n-s-u-m-e. Noting the difference in the pronunciation of the last syllable of the second word, thinking how the two words did not really rhyme. "I'll just sit here in the car," I said when we reached the drugstore.

"The hell you will!" hissed my mother as Billy and Shell ran in ahead to claim the booth by the window. "You can march yourself in there and watch us all enjoy ours! Sniveling like a three-year-old in front of half Tuscaloosa. And if you don't pull up those goddamn socks . . ." The car door slammed behind her.

Inside the drugstore, I slid onto the red vinyl bench to sit beside my brother. I put my hands in my lap. Pearl stopped arranging the new Revlon lipstick display and washed her hands. Her white coat hung loosely on her narrow shoulders, and an inch too much wrist showed at the end of the sleeves. She pulled out her pencil and pad and winked at me. I stopped in to buy spearmint gum almost every day on my way home from school. "Now, what'll it be?"

I glanced up for an instant with red eyes then looked back down, silent. "A double chocolate soda with extra syrup for me," said Billy. "We got shots. They didn't even hurt."

"Bring the baby one scoop of vanilla with strawberries. I'll have a banana split with three cherries. Nothing for this one today." Momma took out her compact and started powdering her nose.

"Lissa cried," Shell said with a mournful look.

Pearl closed her lips tightly and turned to prepare the order, moving fast and jerky, so different from the way she leaned forward easy over the counter when I stopped in with Daddy to buy things for his hunting trips—cigarettes and aftershave and something in a package he covered quickly with his hand before I could see, never counting his change the way my mother always did.

The previous November I had told Pearl about my Christmas play at Alberta Methodist. "You gonna be an angel, sugar?" she had asked me. "You oughta be an angel with those curls of yours."

"No, ma'am. Sara Jayne Mills is the angel. Mrs. Propst says I'm too tall for an angel. Nonie's gonna be Mary. Billy's the wise man with myrrh. I'm the narrator. I start with the part about how there were in the same country shepherds abiding, and I end up with let us pray. It's all right." I added that because I didn't want Pearl feeling sorry for me. "I'm the only one who can reach the pulpit without standing on a peach crate."

"Well, I know you'll be the star, smart as you are. You just stand up tall and talk up loud so everybody can hear you." The night of the pageant, I looked out over the congregation till I found Pearl. Later she told me I made her proud. "Up there like you own cotton in Augusta, missy. And you did not miss a single word."

Pearl stared at my mother from behind the counter. Billy finished his soda with an accidental slurp. Momma glared at him, then resumed daintily lifting the last of her maraschinos to her lips by its stem. Most of the strawberries decorated the front of Shell's dress. I turned to the magazine rack, reading the titles and headlines one after the other. Dag Dies. A Short History of Swearing. Fascination: What It Is and Who Has It. Ford Amazes Car World with Plans for Revolutionary Smallest Compact.

"Somebody should really tell that poor woman not to wear pink lipstick with all that dyed red hair of hers," my mother muttered, rolling her eyes when Pearl turned back to her work. Momma slapped some money on the table and bundled Shell out to the car, telling me to wait for the change.

"You do good tonight in your spelling bee, sugar," Pearl told me, slipping me three tiny lipstick samples with the coins. "I'll be out there rooting for you."

I walked out into the evening and slid into the back seat. "That poor old frump from the drugstore, looking at me like I ate my young. What does she know?" She started a tirade that would last all the way home while I examined the labels on the plastic tubes. Purple Passion, Love That Red, and Honey Bee Pink.

"And I wish to hell it could have been anyone else in town but that busybody Rachel Weaver at that hellhole of a clinic! They'll be laughin' all over Pine Park Circle by tomorrow morning." She stepped out of the car, looking around as if she expected to see the gleeful crowds congregating. "I can just hear them. High-falutin' Marjorie Delbridge getting her younguns free polio shots. To hell with all of them!" In the kitchen, she broke a nail opening her Bufferin bottle. I noticed that she only found one pill in it and she always took three. I ran to the bathroom to see if we had another bottle while Billy scrambled to fetch the high heel that landed behind the sofa.

Billy put on his pajamas and got Shell into hers. Momma had a little over an hour to get me over to the school for the program. My brother and sister would spend the night at the Old House. "Don't tell your grandmother you had ice cream for supper," my mother instructed as she kissed them goodbye. "And Billy? You pick up your sister and carry her. Those chestnut burrs will cut right through her slippers," she hollered as the screen door slammed. She put a pot of water on to boil and splashed in two hot dogs for our supper. I wrapped the buns in tinfoil and lit the oven.

In the bathroom, I tried to get a comb through my hair, failed, and fastened it back with two plastic barrettes that matched my dress. I washed my face and hoped it would pass muster. Probably would, worn out as Momma was. Nothing went right when Daddy took one of his hunting trips and he was almost a week into one now. Momma wrapped our hot dogs in paper towels and I poured the iced tea into Dixie cups. She and I ate in the car, careful not to spill.

She dropped me off at the front door of the school. I ran in ahead to the backstage area and walked out from behind the curtain. The grand piano had been wheeled to the far corner of the stage to make room for the row of wooden chairs where the other contestants sat. I took my seat.

From the stage, I watched my mother enter through the double doors at the back of the auditorium. She paused for a moment, scanning the rows, and spotted a single seat in the second row. She smoothed her skirt and her hair and took the aisle with long, confident strides, chin up and heels clicking as if her feet did not even hurt her. As the auditorium filled, I watched the other mothers enter with their husbands or their friends. Momma opened her program, then glanced around as the lights dimmed and the principal stepped into the spotlight to make her opening speech.

My mother's brow tensed the way it did when she balanced right on the edge of a headache. She closed her eyes against the throbbing. I saw her jerk herself awake from dozing twice, then look to the sides to see if anyone else had noticed. We stood to pledge allegiance. The audience sat, and we began to spell.

As usual, it came down to Rhonda and me.

I could see my mother well, her eyes narrowing whenever her boss's little daughter approached the spotlit microphone. Momma would lean forward, her lips twisted, anticipating an error.

Rhonda repeated the word Mrs. Hamner called out. She began to spell, piping the letters clearly and without hesitation. "T-E-T-N-U-S."

A sad "aww" spewed up from the disappointed crowd. The worst part of watching Rhonda's face was the way her dimples faded, the prettiness of her blush deepening over to something sad. Rhonda left the spotlight and walked back to her chair, flushed with disbelief and embarrassment, her chin quivering in an involuntary way I recognized that nurse's hand on my chin, sharp as scissors to a nail's quick.

The audience became silent as if responding to the sad crinkling of Rhonda's starched petticoats when she sat. I hiked up my socks and stood. I looked down to make sure my hem was not turned up and my slip was not showing. As I passed Rhonda, I touched her shoulder, gave her a soft pat.

With the lights down low I could not distinguish the faces of most of the watchers, but some, I could. Just the ones in the first few rows. I knew most by name and recognized them as friends. Mr. Liggon sat down front, his belly lapping over his Sunday trousers. He helped me cross the street in the morning and sold my mother butter beans at the curb market on Saturday. Beside him sat Jonah, the man who pumped gas at the Shell station and worked second shift part-time with my father at the paper mill. I could not find Pearl, but I knew she was in the room, hoping for me.

I looked out over my neighbors sitting together in the dark. The way their shapes moved slightly, bending in close, then shifting apart, filled me with tenderness for them. The small sounds their bodies made. Their awkward shufflings, their clearing of their throats, and stifled coughs. Their whispered 'scuse me's when their arms or legs inadvertently touched. My own heart thumped fast and hard to be in front of so many, but not from fear. I loved them—and not in spite of their grease-stained hands, their comb-tracked hair, and their scraped-down heels, but all the more for their frailties.

And I could see my mother there, sitting alone. Tall and straight, her shoulders pulled back in her red sweater set, her legs posed in the perfect proper angle, high heels polished to high shine. Beautiful to my eyes, prettier than any other woman there. She nodded slightly at me, winked, and her face relaxed. Her posture softened. She eased back into her chair. Holding me in the strength of her gaze, she raised her chin and almost smiled.

I knew I was not the audience favorite any more than I was her favorite child. Six inches too tall for my age and my dress, front teeth missing for at least four years. Nobody had really combed out my hair all the way in over a week. My Sunday best paled next to Rhonda's red organdy and I could feel the safety pin that held the strap of my cotton slip.

But I knew that word. I knew it even though, for the life of me, I could not recall where I had first learned it. I could see "tetanus" on the page, its silent A smack in the middle. Letters and the words they formed—sometimes they just popped right up in my mind all in a row, the way a crocus will a long time after you've forgotten you planted it. I aimed my face at my mother. I closed my mouth to smile. I stepped forward on the stage till I stood in front of her, right in the center of that tight golden circle of light.

Gun and Bait

On the way to eat venison chili at the home of one of his girlfriends, my father confessed that he and my mother couldn't stand the sight of each other anymore and had decided to divorce. Whenever he had something important to tell me, Daddy'd say, "C'mon, baby," and hand me the car keys. He'd sip and give directions till the blacktop ended and we rode on dirt and gravel. I took a pull of whiskey from the flask he offered, passed it back to him, and drove his Cadillac off the muddy road and into a muddier ditch. Fortunately, we both wore seatbelts and I was driving slowly, as it was nighttime and raining and I did not know how the hell to get to Lorreen's. Daddy pulled me out the passenger door since my side lay on the ground. Once he'd established that I had not been injured, we started trudging the mile to Lorreen's house, hand in hand. "You still gonna love me?"

"That won't never stop," he replied, knowing without my saying so that I meant after I wrecked his car rather than after the divorce. Long ago used to my here-today-gone-tomorrow father, I felt confident that not much would change.

I apologized about his prized Cadillac. That one was maroon with white leather upholstery. "Aw, hell, baby," he replied. "Won't be no harm done. Me and Fritz'll get Kenny's tractor tomorrow and pull it right out. Anybody asks tonight, I swerved to miss a deer." At the time I thought it the most gallant thing I had ever heard. In retrospect, I realize he said it because we were celebrating my eleventh birthday that night.

Most of my librarian colleagues at Duke University would probably be afraid of most of my relatives. To be honest, I can't blame them. Shaking hands with a couple of my cousins in broad daylight is enough to make you sleep with the lights on till Groundhog Day.

Daddy's a different story, though. Despite his occasional run-in with the authorities and his deep and abiding belief that all sentient beings should carry loaded pistols, the man could flat-out charm. So let's be fair. His legal problems usually had to do with the finer points of arms-bearing; something he said when he got thanked for not smoking; or the way he drove cars and women—the former way too fast and the latter damn near crazy.

I thought about my father, after I finished graduate school, when big alligators wandered into the parking lot of my apartment building in Baton Rouge from the Bayou de Plantier across the road. You'd step on the little ones right often. It hurt me to see them, car-mashed, usually dead, about a foot long, max. I worked in the Special Collections Library at LSU then, and I would find what was left in the morning, dried flat and already soldered to sun-warmed Louisiana asphalt, looking like retreads from a tricycle blowout.

Didn't see the big ones much. Adult alligators, unlike us, get smarter and shyer with time and experience. Once in a while, though, a big one would slither out of the mud and cross Lee Drive by night, seduced by a resident corgi's scent or by a three-day leftover étouffée ripening in the dumpster. There would be shouts, squeals, car lights, flashlights, and finally, blue lights. Men would come armed with darts, guns, long loops on sticks, and big ideas. A couple of times they actually managed to capture or kill the outraged creature without hurting themselves.

More often he'd lunge and his tormenters would shriek and cuss and jump back further than you'd think they could—hell, further than they thought they could—and then, he'd take his time, lumbering on back to the bayou where he could be his reptilian self without getting in trouble.

And that's when I'd think about Daddy. Easy-going and slow to anger in his element, once in a while he'd just venture out too far, get caught in the headlights of more refined and genteel folks and simply scare the living shit out of them. Don't get me wrong. The way he saw it, Daddy never actually broke the law. He simply never allowed it to break him. He tripped over it sometimes, the way he might an obstacle in his path. He looked at it—confused, annoyed, embarrassed if people were watching, maybe a little bruised if he stumbled hard enough—and wondered how the hell that got in his way. He might feel foolish for not avoiding it. Never once would it occur to him to blame himself.

After years of aggravation and surrender, my parents went down to the Tuscaloosa County courthouse and got divorced. My mother had always hated Daddy's hunting, hated the guts and the guns of it, hated the gamy roasts soaking in buttermilk in her white kitchen sink. Hated the sight of her curly-headed eldest daughter all bloody and laughing, holding a buck's hoof in her hand and yanking on the naked white tendon to watch it contract. Hated the call from the teacher when the girl took said hoof to show-and-tell.

Most of all she hated him leaving her alone for his woods and his wildness, and especially for the times he said he'd left her for them, but come back home with no carcass on the hood, humming a popular new song and how the hell could he have heard it down there in West Greene, Alabama, with no radio in the cabin or the goddamn truck? Hard to tell when it shifted, but before long it was the hunter she hated instead of the hunt.

But that took some time, and no damn wonder. My favorite picture of him hangs in my study. He was thirty-six years old when it was taken. His pride's nearly popping the buttons off his flannel shirt. He holds up the giant buck's lifeless head so lightly, like he's leading it in a dance, the animal more moose than deer. Some of his buddies say it still holds an Alabama record. Antlers spread out like banners in a breeze. And there's my father smiling, not at the camera, but over the photographer's shoulder at the my-my-my-ing all the women would do, and at the head-shaking of the jealous men who would spit on the ground at the span of that rack. Daddy's chin thrust out to here and him grinning like whatever's coming up next, he's ready and waiting for it.

I saw that grin again in an unexpected place sometime in the 1970s. Might have been my freshman year at the University of Alabama. Annie and I were sharing a joint on a screened porch in a rainstorm while she taught me to read my new Tarot cards, me rhyming it with carrot the first time I said it out loud. I pulled a card and there he was.

The card portrayed a young man stepping out boldly, smiling up at the sky with complete confidence and optimism. The pack on his back indicates that he is beginning a journey. What he does not know is that he is about a baby step away from a cliff. No matter, though.

His little dog is with him, pulling him from the brink with a tug on his ankle.

Card turns up in a positive reading, it symbolizes many things. Innocence. Novel experiences. Adventure. Freedom and excitement. Trust. Lack of inhibition. Faith in spite of danger. Upside down, we're talking real bad. Impulsiveness. Irresponsibility. Wasted energy. Caution to the wind and honey, you're playing with fire. Taking unnecessary risks without considering one's effect on others. The inscription below the rendering reads "The Fool."

Now that all depends on how you look at him, and believe me, over the years I've looked at my father from every angle. I have to agree with all the people who loved him, and those who despised him weren't too far off the money. After my mother had had it up to here and moved us across town in the middle of the night, Daddy tried to convince her to take him back—first with candy and flowers, then with apologies and big fancy boxes of My Sin perfume including the bath products, but none of it took. I'd find his offerings on the back-door stoop when I came home from school. I would sniff them like a collie pup if they were wrapped or taste them if they weren't, then set them on the kitchen counter where they'd stay till my mother got home from her job. From where I sat in my room doing my homework, I heard her kick off her high heels and slam his gifts into the trashcan.

About this time the hunting photograph came out in the *Tuscaloosa News*. I got temporarily famous for being Big George Delbridge's daughter. Three older boys, none of whom had ever shown any interest in me at all, vied for my attention in the lunchroom for several days before I told them to leave me the hell alone, that my parents were divorced and invitations to Greene County hunting clubs would not be forthcoming.

When Daddy got the rack back from the taxidermist and hung it up out at the cabin at River Bend, the damned thing took up a third of the room for all of ten minutes before the weight of it took down the cabin's interior wall. Daddy and his brother hauled off the rubble and rebuilt it within a week, and convinced my father's friend Jesse to keep the head mount for him for a while. Jesse's wife had recently run him off and sent him to live in that new complex down by the bowling alley—the one with cinder-block painted walls. After Jesse moved in with the 7-Eleven night clerk, Daddy laid it on the floor of Uncle John's garage where it spent a few years as a moth hatchery, staring up at the ceiling like it was biding its time.

And I kept waiting for my mother to take him back. I had seen her do it many times, and even as a child I understood why. For one thing, he smelled better than anyone else on earth—like wood smoke and good whiskey muddled up with something fresh and green—and that Fool-smile was something worth seeing. Unfortunately, everything caught his attention equally. You could never bank on him looking your way for very long, not even if you were his offspring. When his eyes finally rested on me, though, I knew without doubt that for those minutes I was the only thing he saw, and I knew my father loved me. He would just pour his heart out unfiltered through his gaze in a way I've never seen another man do.

I also knew that it would have to last. Come morning, he might be gone again. He disappeared for days, weeks, or months—once for a year or so—hunting and drinking and gallivanting around. Count on his love, I learned, but never his presence.

My parents did not believe in amiable separations. They would not give each other the time of day or a running start. After the divorce, I never saw my parents in the same room again. When I'd almost get used to Daddy being gone he'd turn up again one morning like some one-eared tomcat everybody'd given up on. Not being one to adhere to a steady court-ordained visitation schedule, he would drive up and honk the horn in the driveway when he got to feeling paternal, and I'd go running out. My mother dog-cussed him, but found it simpler to write a note telling the teacher I was sick than to argue. You had to get up close and look at him to argue effectively. She never once went to that door. "Hurry up," she'd holler. "It's your goddamn father!" I'd grab my coat and run.

And he would keep me out of school for the day for something wonderful: to go see newborn twin Charolais calves down in Eutaw; to visit a nineteenth-century baby's grave he'd found in the woods with the words "Gone so soon" chipped onto a crude little stone by someone with a broken heart; or to drive out into the Sipsey swamp to pick wild muscadines for Kenny to mash into wine.

One morning in March before the divorce, maybe second grade or so, before the spring had warmed up good, Daddy woke me up early and took me down to West Greene to his small barn and his hunting cabin. We stopped by Kenny's on the way, and I watched sunrise from the seat of the borrowed tractor, buttoned into my father's jacket with him, cheeks chapping in the early chill, riding in his lap down a red dirt road to the field where he planted soybeans for his cattle. Once we reached his land on the bank of the Black Warrior River, he dangled me off the seat by one arm till my school shoes touched the ground, turned the tractor, then lowered the blade while I stood still, inhaling the loam scent of its first slice into the soil. He told me to wait till he was two cow-lengths ahead, then to follow, watching the turned earth for anything not dirt.

Most of what I saw shining were rocks—quartz or sandstone. I found one tooth from a dead deer or farm animal, and a cracked bottle that had once been full of something nobody had made for a hundred years.

Then, pretty as a ruby in a jeweler's window, my treasure appeared on top of a red dirt clod the size of my head. An intact spearhead, thick and around an inch and a half long, a smooth red-tan color. Both sides still sharp enough to cut. Tiny indentations where the long-dead maker had chipped off flecks formed a scalloped edge. Knowing the danger of approaching the tractor and knowing that even if I called him, my father would not hear me over the roar around us, I kept my beautiful prize deep in my pocket, checking first for holes. For the next two hours, I followed him through the field, waiting more than searching, clutching it safe in my dirty palm in my pocket. The spearhead, plump as a heart, drew and held my own warmth like something alive.

Daddy finally cut the tractor's engine, and river sounds, softer in the din's absence, and birdsong picked right up in its place. "Pretty one, baby," my father said when I placed my treasure in his hand. He smiled at me. "You keep that all your life."

On the way home we stopped in at a country store to buy me a Dr Pepper, and he lifted me onto the counter to sit while his hunting buddies made a fuss over my find and me. "This little split-tail spotted it in the dirt behind a tractor down there at West Green. Got good eyes just like her Daddy. Pretty ones, too," he bragged, winking at me, and every ballet recital he had ever missed lost all significance.

Three years later, when the archaeologists from the University of Alabama began their dig at West Green, they asked to see the artifacts we had found over the years. They marveled over my spearhead, not because of its beauty, but because it was of a stone not found in the region, thus indicating that the Creeks either traded up and down the river or migrated from somewhere else. They tried to get me to give them my spearhead, offering first a transistor radio, then a plaque with my name on it, then a picnic party at Moundville State Park for ten of my friends and me. The archaeologist turned to my father for help.

"You heard her," Daddy shrugged. "Stubborn as a jenny mule and her momma rolled into one. Hell, I never could do a thing with either one of them." He rose and took my hand, and the interview was over.

My father and I passed a good portion of our time together on that river he loved so much. We'd come home with a stringer full of bream my mother would cuss about having to clean. After they divorced I'd spend the night at the cabin with Daddy and some red-headed woman I promised not to mention to anyone. She'd brush out my hair in front of the fire at night and tell me stories about Conjure Wives and Bloody Bones. In the morning we'd all eat fresh catfish skillet-fried in bacon grease on a wood stove.

People would row, troll, and ski on the Black Warror looking for fun or fish. Sometimes somebody from the county would go out onto that tarry moccasin-heaven of a river, and sometimes they'd go into it due to accident, drink, despair, or some unfortunate combination of the three. Once in a while they did not come back up. When the boat floated to shore in one piece or several, the police or the sheriff would call my great-uncle Bob, who dove rescue and recovery for the Tuscaloosa fire department. If the boat looked bad, Daddy'd suit up with him. My cousin Bobby watched them several times. He told me they'd mark out the river in sections with cable, then dive and surface, dive and surface, move the cable and do it all again. Finally one of our fathers would come back up, wade ashore yanking off the mask without speaking and stand there breathing fresh air with his eyes closed tight and his hands on his hips. When the other saw him like that on the banks, he'd join him. They'd send Bobby to wait in the rescue truck. The men would speak together, quiet and alone, shaking their heads and pointing and touching one another's shoulders. They talked about what waited for them in the river, then one would radio the coroner before they went back in to fish out the body or what they'd found of it.

Sometimes a few days had passed by the time they discovered the corpse, giving the catfish time to have a go at it. They'd net whatever the creatures had left and haul it in, bits of the boater oozing through the net and souping up the water as it came. Daddy would come home with his jaw muscles working, stay in the shower for a long time. If he went to bed then, we had to tiptoe like he'd been working third shift. Most times, though, he'd walk out back to the peach trees without saying a word. Once when I was ten, I fetched the Turkey bottle from under the driver's seat out to the orchard without being asked. When I held it out to him, he grabbed me like he had to save me from falling and squeezed me to his chest so tightly I coughed. He eased up, but didn't let go.

The bottle hit the dirt. His body shook, although I never saw one tear, and he croaked to me, "Baby, that boy wudn't but eleven years old."

"Who was he, Daddy?"

"You wouldn't know him, baby. Little colored boy." He held me to him for a long time, and I swear now I could still smell river under Lifebuoy soap until he bent to retrieve the bottle.

By the time I was in college, Gulf States Paper Company had closed down. Daddy had a new career, one that suited him. He bought into a store way out in Greene County and set up an apartment in the back. During the day, he ran the register and played cards. Evenings, he doubled as the live-in night watchman. Nobody could advise hunting and fishing customers on their bait and ammo better than he could.

Louise, Kenny's wife, brought Daddy his lunch every day. He liked his big meal at noon. She'd pile dumplings, okra, squash casserole, rice and gravy, speckled butter beans, and a pork chop or two, or maybe a chunk of smoked ham on a Melmac plate with the wheat design Brillo-scrubbed to streaks. Top it off with a couple of cornsticks crisped up just right to soak up the drippings and wrap it all up in tinfoil. She'd walk down the highway from her cleaning job at the Applegates' house to deliver. Daddy and Glory, the stock clerk, sat on the secondhand plaid sofa together if they were alone, watching *The Young and the Restless,* him with his platter and her with her microwaved Lean

Cuisine. They ate with plastic utensils. Whenever they heard tires on the gravel, he jumped up like he'd gotten caught in flagrante delicto. Not wanting to start any talk around town about him and a colored girl, he'd eat standing behind the counter till he rang up the customer and they left. Once they drove off, he'd come back to the couch, bringing a plate of ripe tomatoes they grew out back. He sliced them thick and offered Glory the dish like he'd offer an apology, then ask her what he'd missed.

Kenny and Louise lived rent-free in a cabin on Daddy's land, took care of his hunting dogs, did a little truck farming, kept a few beehives. Daddy liked to pick Kenny up in the summer to fish and in the autumn to hunt. Kenny, he told me, was a damn good shot and knew the best places. When he hunted with Kenny, only the two of them went, leaving early and coming back the same day. Long hunts with other white men meant Daddy'd stay overnight at the club, and Kenny would stay back at his place, come when the white men returned to help finish cleaning the kill, to put up and feed the dogs if it was bird season, and to get the fire ready for the barbecue. Good people, Daddy called Kenny and Louise, and once he even called Sam Marshall to help get their son Jo-Jo a job at the catfish farm when he came back from Vietnam.

After I'd finished college and moved up to North Carolina, I never knew he was coming to visit till he was a few blocks from my house. He'd do this a couple of times a year. The notion of visiting me might start with some bragging around the card table he and a hunting crony and a retired football coach and some guy who owned an army surplus store had set up by the cash register of the country store/gas station/ bait-and-gun shop/video rental in Greene County, Alabama.

Often he bragged about me, his oldest girl, the one who had herself a master's degree and worked up at Duke University, up there in the library with all those old letters and diaries. Didn't you see that Civil War special? The one with the music, the one that told the Northern side? My girl's stuff, most of that was. He'd pull a twenty-year-old picture out of his wallet, play one more hand, and before he knew it, there he was on 85 North with a full tank of premium, Wild Turkey on the front seat and satchel on the back. No warning, no "Baby-is-this-a-good-time?" Invite a few friends, he'd tell me on the phone from a BP station a block from my house. Invite some pretty ones.

I'd drag a comb through the worst of the tangles, maybe have a minute to smear on some lipstick—something bright I thought he'd like—before I heard him blast the car horn from the parking lot of the Baptist church across the street. He did this to be polite. Daddy believed you shouldn't sneak up on people if you have good manners or good sense.

From my window I watched my father unfold all six feet of himself from the Adriatic blue Brougham, his fifth of Turkey two inches short of empty in his left hand and his pistol in his right. Ambidextrous when it came to whiskey, Daddy only trusted his right hand to shoot. He ambled to the curb, stopped, looked both ways like a good schoolboy before crossing.

Plans for his evening did not include shooting. He carried the gun out of habit, so used to its weight that sometimes he looked for it when it was right there in his shoulder holster, the way a woman looks for the glasses stuck up on her head. He had just driven six hundred miles to treat me to dinner.

I'd meet him in the front yard, taking the gun from his hand when I broke his breath-stealer of a hug. I'd savor the pull of brown liquor I drew from the bottle he offered and stash the gun safe in the sideboard till morning. Dinner would be rich, his treat. We'd go to a steakhouse and order lamb and suck the bones dry. My father would charm my friends and the waitress. We would close down the restaurant, invite everyone to my house for drinks around the kitchen table. Daddy might blow a few card tricks that night, but never one joke, and by the time they said goodnight, my friends would love him too much to tell him they had chosen the five of clubs, not the ace of spades. Love him enough to express amazement and ignore his mistakes, no matter what he did. He'd drive back early so he could do the evening shift at the store.

For the most part, living behind his place of employment worked out pretty well for my father. He did have a narrow escape when the first store in Lewiston burned down. He barely had time to get out with his laundry basket and seven pairs of cowboy boots. Twice he thwarted robbery attempts. An article in the November 1990 issue of the *Sportsman's Journal* published in York, Alabama, told of one of these adventures.

On September 27, my father was dead to the world in his apartment behind the Eutaw Bait and Gun Shop when all hell broke lose. He heard an ungodly crash of breaking glass and falling masonry and ran out firing his 9-mm pistol at two robbers he found throwing guns and ammunition into the back of a stolen Chevrolet Blazer. They had driven it right through the plate glass window in the front of the store. "You can't move on a concrete floor full of glass when you're barefooted," my father informed the reporter. "I didn't have time to be scared."

Unfortunately, Daddy did not have time for clothes, either. The Eutaw police arrived two minutes after the thieves fled. They were apprehended later, and the headline read "Naked Gun Surprises Brazen Robbers." Although his bullets missed their human targets, Daddy did manage to severely wound a new truck in the Odum Chevrolet automotive dealership lot across the street. One of the salespeople took to calling Daddy to inform him whenever a new shipment of targets arrived.

The other failed robbery happened a few years earlier at the Lewisburg store before it burned. Daddy and Glory were watching *General Hospital* when a young man with a stocking over his head came in and grabbed Glory by the neck, holding a gun to her head and demanding the money in the register. My father flipped the sofa backwards, knocking the man to the floor. The gun went flying across the room and Glory grabbed it and ran to the phone.

When the police arrived, my father was still beating on the man, who had ceased to struggle. They pulled the stocking off his bloody face, and Daddy saw that it was Jo-Jo, Kenny and Louise's son. He spent a few days in Druid City Hospital's intensive care ward before his arrest.

Louise did not bring my father's lunch for a few days, forcing him to subsist on hot dogs and Frostees. When she came with the plate the following Monday, her head was bowed down. "I'm so sorry, Mister George, and after all you done for us. Jo-Jo ain't been right since he come back from overseas."

"Don't you worry about it, Louise. Lotsa good boys come back like that." He took a smoked wild turkey breast out of the deep freeze and put it in a bag for her. "If I'da known it was your Jo-Jo, I wouldn't have kept on hitting him so hard." Poor old Kenny died within a year of the incident, like he couldn't abide the shame. And my father took a venison haunch to Louise every time he got a deer until his death in 1996.

I lived in Montgomery in the mid-eighties, and called Daddy one Friday to ask if he would accompany me to Gates' Lodge for some prime rib. The restaurant was ten miles from everywhere and the county was dry, but you could bring your own bottle and the waitress would bring your setups. Daddy handed me the keys, and I started the Cadillac—a black one this year. It being a football weekend, the traffic was steady.

On a two-lane gravel road, the car in front of me stopped with no warning. I braked just in time to avoid contact, as did the car behind me. We sat for about five minutes, taking the occasional sip of Turkey.

"Baby?" said Daddy, taking a photograph out of his wallet. "You remember Louann Rider from out in Cottondale? She was that old gal I took to my class reunion three years ago?" I didn't, but I said I did.

"Well, baby, I messed up and married her. Don't know what I was thinking. Hell, I probably wasn't. This summer I went down to Pensacola snapper fishing with your Aunt Berenice, and when I come back, baby, she had flat cleaned me out. Took the furniture, took my truck, took my money, took my goddamn home entertainment center. Took my guns. Worst of it was that she took my big deer rack, too.

"So I got me a detective. Traced her up to Toccoa, Georgia. You should have seen her face when she turned on the porch light. I told her she could have the furniture, half the money, and even my truck if she could make the payments. I gave her two of the guns, but I had me a U-Haul waiting in the drive, and I brought that rack back down to Montgomery and hung it up in your second cousin's barbecue restaurant. You get back home tomorrow, go on by there and tell him whose girl you are. I guarantee you won't pay for your pig."

I thanked him and took down the directions to the restaurant. Took another hit of whiskey and we got out of the car to see what the holdup was.

About a quarter of a mile ahead, a police car had blocked off the road. The officer and my father nodded to each other.

"George."

"Earl."

"We got us a mess here," the policeman explained, and I could see the truth of what he said. A black angus cow lay on her side in the middle of the road, bellowing up to heaven, two legs broken bad and bleeding from around her ribcage into the gravel. The woman who had been driving the truck had not seen her wandering around. What they were all doing was waiting for the injured beast to die.

Any person who grew up in Alabama when I did knew that the decent thing to do was to shoot the poor creature and shoot it fast. They'd also know that was the thing you could not do unless the cow was yours or you'd end up paying the owner twice what she was worth on the hoof. Police couldn't shoot her without the owner's consent. And nobody would claim her because they'd wind up paying a fine for letting her wander as well as paying for damage to the woman's truck.

Daddy looked at his watch, then put his arm around the policeman. Smiling widely, he confided, "Earl, I'm not sure, but I believe I saw an old lady consuming an alcoholic beverage in her car about a quarter mile back. Think you might ought to walk back and check on her?"

Earl hesitated for a moment, then nodded seriously. "I believe I'll do that, George. Always want to uphold the law. Yes, indeed."

As soon as Earl had walked away, Daddy took off his jacket and handed me his pistol. He then removed his shoulder holster and his shirt, giving them to me to hold. He took the gun and knelt bare-chested at the head of the terrified animal, stroking her neck. "Turn your head, baby," he told me, and fired. Something warm and wet hit me on the leg. When I bent over in the brambles to vomit, I felt my father's hand holding back my hair, and I had not even asked him to.

I never made it to the barbecue restaurant in Montgomery. I meant to, but to be honest, I was more of a quiche-eater when I was not with my father. For the next five years, the head of Daddy's buck hung on the heavy-beamed wall until the night the grill caught fire and burned the whole damn place down. You wouldn't think two chunks of bone that big would go to ash like that, but they sure as hell will. Daddy cried like a baby when he called to tell me.

He always blamed Louann for that loss, but blame was on him, too. He married too often and way too quickly. It's just the way he was. I knew about a few of his holy unions besides the one that pro-duced us: one right after my mother divorced him to Jean, a pretty woman with three natural gas wells and black hair long enough for her to sit on; and one to the mother of a school chum of my little sister. And there isn't time or room here for me to even start on the ones he didn't marry, the ones who came up to me my first year of college at the University of Alabama after hearing the professor call the roll, simpering, trilling "Ooooo, are you George's daughter?"

I found out about my father's first wife the year I turned twelve. By then his marriage to my mother had run its course and I suppose he'd started in contemplating number three.

I was sitting on my grandmother's davenport where the air conditioning would hit me square, going through a shoebox full of family photographs when I found it. Daddy in black and white, looking way too young for his Navy uniform, leaning on an old car parked by a dried-up cornfield. The Ford sported a tail of tin cans. Misspelled just-married jokes dripped down the fenders, front and back. The blonde on his arm was not my mother.

By the date on the bottom of the deckle-edged snapshot, I figured my father at seventeen. He told me years later he had gotten a note from my grandfather so the Navy would take him.

I held it out to Grandma. She fumbled for her bifocals without looking away from *The Price is Right*. Once she situated them square on her nose, she glanced over, then snatched the photograph so fast the Chihuahua jumped off her lap.

"Your daddy wasn't nothing but a boy. Just a sweet, sweet, stupid boy didn't know no better," she muttered. "Don't you ever bring this up again. Now you go get Grandma some iced tea." She set her glasses back on the coffee table and rubbed her eyes like what I had showed her just about set them on fire.

His second marriage produced my brother, then me, then my sister. My mother stuck it out for fourteen years and three and a half pregnancies before she'd had enough of his absence, his cheating, and the charm of his apologies.

Last time he handed me his car keys was the year he died. I knew I was in for a humdinger when he told me to pull over. I braced myself, and as I sat with him in his navy blue Brougham parked on a dirt road in Ralph, Alabama, my father showed me the x-rays. His lungs, the doctor told him, looked like lace.

I had to agree. The plate Daddy showed me reminded me of a black-and-white-photograph of amputated angel wings. "Damn paper mill finally knocked the wind out of me, baby," was how my father put it between coughs. He recollected the day they had brought in those enormous asbestos vats, his pride in being the foreman. Forty years later, twenty-four of his thirty former employees were diagnosed. Daddy's case was one of the worst, aggravated by his daily pack of Winstons.

Then, at his direction, I drove him out to the Black Warrior River to where a tall man about ten years my senior stood smoking beside a dirty blue Dodge Ram. My father introduced me to the primary reason for his marriage to that woman he had his arm around in the just-married picture. Daddy said, "Sugar, this is your brother. I wasn't around much when he was growing up, but one time I took you to watch him play football for County High." I did not remember this, but I smiled politely and extended my hand.

I wish I could tell you that Ed became my friend, or at least that we hit it off. Turns out my sorry half-brother Ed owned a nursing home I hope nobody ever puts me in. You either. Right before Daddy died, the same day he sold me his Cadillac for a dollar, he told me Ed owed him twenty-two thousand dollars for a land deal and gave me the promissory note.

My brother and sister and I tried to do right by Ed. We included him when we could, putting his name in the obituary with ours despite the fact that I had found legal papers with which my father's marriage to the blonde had been annulled and he had relinquished all claim to the baby boy so his mother could marry the man Grandma said was Ed's real father and change Ed's name to Bivins.

Ed embarrassed us all by coming drunk to the viewing. Many of the visitors were Methodist ladies who had taught me in Sunday school when I was little girl. Ed stood chain-smoking in Banlon shirtsleeves outside the front door of the funeral parlor. When I went out to get some air, he complained to me that everyone in my family was staring at him like they would a whore in church. He put his arm around my shoulder and confided that he considered me to be the pick of the litter. I shrugged him off like a bug that had lit on my arm and went inside and stood by my grandma. She never once turned her head to look his way.

When we gently suggested to Ed a few months after the funeral that he should start making monthly payments into the estate account, he looked me in the eye and swore that he'd already paid back every penny to my father in cash. Ed never showed again after we put Daddy in the ground, and he never paid us his share for the flowers on Daddy's casket, an expense traditionally shared by the children of the deceased.

I have felt sorry for my half-brother since, but I just never knew what to do about that sorrow. I guess he owes us twenty-two thousand and seventy-five dollars, but we won't ever see it. Without a word Ed and my family somehow agreed to not bother each other anymore. He got the money and we got Daddy for a long time. Most days, the way I figure, we got the better end of the deal.

My mother did not attend the funeral, but I found her that evening crying with her face in one of his shirts from the laundry basket I brought home after cleaning out his house. I guess she was trying to catch whatever was left of him. Daddy died without a will, of course, and by the time we wandered through a petting zoo of probate court officials, ex-wives, outside children, a red-headed girlfriend half his age, and an Alabama funeral director with two alimony payments, there wasn't a lot left. I got a few of his shirts that I sleep in when I have the blues and three pairs of his cowboy boots. We sold the Cadillac and split the money three ways. My brother got his gun collection except for his favorite, the pre–World War II Walther 9-mm Banner pistol, which my sister took for her son. Too bad, because he's not the type to care about guns. He was on the high side of ten before my sister would let him cross the street alone. Doesn't recognize a shirt as a shirt unless it has a polo player stitched on it.

I got two photographs that hung on my daddy's wall. The one of the deer and this other one. In it, my father stands by a pile of stones and busted-up lumber mess that had been his family's home the day before. The tornado of 1932 had just careened through Samantha, Alabama, and taken off with everything worth having. My grandmother told me about the day it happened: she could not get the dress pattern she was trying to cut to lay flat on the kitchen table, it was so windy. She got up to close the window, and the next thing she remembered she was digging through the pile of splintered wood, hollering for her three children. They were safe, thank the Lord, although the right side of my father's face was swollen up twice its size. My grandmother looked down and saw that her shoe had disappeared from her left foot. Two days later, the neighbor's collie dog brought it up on the front porch of the house where she was staying with a friend from her church. In the photograph, my father wears an aviator cap with earflaps and holds his cat Bootie in his arms, legs all dangling down. He was only five years old, but there was that heartbreak of a smile, and his whole house rubble.

Sometimes his death seems like just another one of his abrupt departures, and I halfway expect him to show up—handsome, all kisses and jokes and whiskey and trouble—charming and exasperating everybody one more time. And I see the ways I'm like him.

Give me a choice to this day and I'll take the Cadillac over the Mini Cooper. Deal me in at the poker table, I'll raise on a bluff and I'll pass on your church social. Have my fun and make amends later if I can. Most times I can. Smile and charm away the traffic ticket, wiggle free of the tight spot. Laugh harder than anyone else at my own jokes.

And no matter what kind of trouble comes up, all it takes to make myself safe is to close my eyes, conjure his hand in mine on a dark Alabama dirt road. George Riley Delbridge died ten years ago this month of a cancer that hid till too late and ate him up fast, lungs first, but you can't really lose anybody you love like that. Love a man like that once and you never get shed of him. You forget crying your pillow soggy the night he never came to take you to the fair and remember only the next morning, waking up in a room full of red teddy bears. Look for him in every man who catches your eye. They lack that smile so the pull can't hold. Your eye starts to wander before too long.

I'm so happy still whenever the man comes back. He helps me all the time. Sticks a little check from his class action suit into my mailbox right when I need a vacation. Hides my keys when I'm too drunk to drive. Sometimes my father makes me laugh, and others, he shadows me, breath on my back, but let me tell you something true: I can count on my father now in ways I never could before. He's right there, giving me a hint, calling me back, goading me to go ahead, take a chance when I need to. If I ever get too close, I know that's him at my heel, tugging me away from the edge. This never stops.

Faith of Our Fathers

differed from the majority of Tuscaloosa children in a couple of significant ways. My mother did not make or serve sweet tea, preferring to sugar her own beverage, and I was not raised Baptist. We did attend a Baptist church for a while when Momma played piano for them, and after she remarried we went to one steady for a year or two, but mostly to help my stepfather's pest control business. He figured Baptists would be more likely to have bug problems than Episcopalians. I even got dunked a time or two during that stint, but I don't think it took.

My real father did not like the Southern Baptist Church. He wouldn't even let me go to Sunbeams with my next-door neighbor when I was five years old. I never was sure why. Baptists aren't supposed to drink, and if they do they won't meet your eye in the liquor store. They don't dance either. Daddy certainly did like doing both, but I don't think that was the reason for his antipathy. After all, he didn't mind Holy Rollers. He let me go to vacation bible school at the Church of the Nazarene down the road, and they didn't even believe in lipstick or women's kneecaps.

Something about him and the Baptists, though. If I pointed out the Baptist minister walking down the street, Daddy would spit on the sidewalk and growl, "I wouldn't piss in his ear if his head was on fire." I never did learn why he harbored such sectarian malice. I asked him several times over the years, and he always came up with a different reason.

Once I was sitting in his back seat, riding out to eat catfish with him and some party gal whose cosmetic franchise he'd bankrolled. "Daddy?" I asked. "What is it with you and the Baptists? Why do you hate them so bad?"

"Baby," he said, shaking his head with regret, "I got kicked out of the Baptist Church a long time ago."

"What for?"

He sat silent till we stopped at the red light. "Falling in love with the preacher's wife."

I scowled at him, dubious. He winked at the blonde sitting next to him.

"I did, sugar. I swear it. We were going at it standing up in the choir room and he walked in without knocking. Kicked us both out. Thought we were dancing." I shooed my hand at him and his girlfriend howled. I knew he'd told the story for her, not me, but I laughed too. Just to be polite. Even at fourteen, I knew that old joke.

On his mother's side, my father descended from generations of Hardshell Baptists. Originally a derogatory name for Primitive Baptists, the term refers to the sect's refusal to budge when it comes to the literal interpretation of the King James Version of the Bible. They believe in predestination. His mother's family had worshiped at Nazareth Primitive Baptist Church in Samantha, Alabama. Like many churches of the denomination, the simple white frame church had two front doors, the left for women and children and the right for men. No piano, as the Bible never mentioned one of those.

The second time I tried to glean information about my father's abhorrence of things Baptist, I was sitting on the front porch swing at my grandma's house, shelling purple-hull peas with my Aunt Mike. Daddy leaned on the railing sipping a longneck Pabst. "Daddy," I said, "I'm supposed to write a report for social studies about my family's religious history. What do you remember about services at Nazareth when you were a boy?"

"Shoot, baby. Not much to tell. Just a lot of damnation and footwashing." Seeing my disappointment, he added, "There was this one all-day preaching I recall, though . . ." And he took off.

"Every single Hardshell man, woman, and child in Tuscaloosa County come out to hear old Brother Willis preach, and several came from far away as Pickens and Bibb. And that was before everybody had a car, too. The Reverend was famous on the Alabama circuit.

"He'd brought with him a man who used to weigh 426 pounds till he gave up the sin of gluttony after hearing Brother Willis expostulating from Proverbs about how you ought to just put a knife to your throat if you're given to appetite. Man said the Lord saved his life by whittling him down to a forty-two-inch waistline. The whole congregation started hollering and praising Jesus' name and seventeen people went on a diet that very hour."

Aunt Mike stopped shelling for a minute. She shook the peas down to the bottom of the pan and threw a handful of shells into a paper bag, rolling her eyes at me.

"After that, he called on a woman—good-looking woman. Said she was a converted Cajun prostitute. She witnessed about how Jesus had rescued her from a life of sin and despair, singing blues and drinking brown liquor and taking up with a different man every day of the week and sometimes two on Saturday night. Said she'd heard Brother Willis preaching about the lips of a strange woman being like a honeycomb and everything else just as smooth as oil . . ."

Aunt Mike interrupted, quoting scripture. "But her end is bitter as wormwood . . ."

"Looked pretty sweet to me," Daddy smirked.

"Sharp as a two-edged sword!" Aunt Mike glared at him, and my father nodded.

"She was sharp, all right. Anyway, honey, she testified that Jesus turned her life around and there she was, out reeling in evildoers all over the South.

"And the women! Honey, I mean to tell you she had every woman in that congregation in tears. They fell all over each other, just repenting and renunciating and twenty-two of them rededicated theirselves to doing right and living God's will."

"George Riley Delbridge, you know you are telling a bold-faced lie!" Aunt Mike's patience was beginning to slip. "Nazareth's Primitive. We don't believe in rededicating!"

"Will you let me tell my story?!" Daddy threw his bottle into the pea-shell bag and fished another beer out of the porch cooler.

"It was coming on evening by then. We sang Old Hundred and gave thanks and some of the sisters laid out a spread on those picnic tables out in the shade. You would not have believed the food. Smoked hams, fried chicken, every kind of green. I counted seven plates of deviled eggs. And they had outdone theirselves on desserts—banana puddings and Lane cakes and lemon icebox pies. We ate ourselves nearly 'bout sick.

"Then Brother Willis reached into the cab of his pickup and pulled out a guitar with a busted string and started playing some songs that woman remembered from New Orleans. She chimed in and about that time old Joe Hardy popped a couple of gallon jugs of Parcus moonshine from up in Madison County and started passing. And by the time the singing was over, people went to pairing off and holding hands and wandering off into that cornfield out by the church, and baby . . ."

He paused, looking me dead-on sincere and shaking his head for emphasis.

"I woke up on the wagon bed the next morning and damned if them Hardshell Baptists hadn't fornicated that cornfield flat!" He moved his hands across an invisible plane, like he was smoothing down a tablecloth. "You put that in your report, baby." He winked.

Aunt Mike jumped up so fast she nearly dumped me and the purple-hulls on the floor. She slapped my father on the arm and went inside, slamming the screen behind her.

I realized that evening that Daddy'd never tell me the truth about this, that my asking just cued him to start pulling my leg with another one of his anti-Baptist yarns.

After that, I asked him more often. Over the years, he told me some doozies.

The last time, I didn't have to ask. I was driving him in his Cadillac with his oxygen tank propped up in the back seat. He wanted to see how high the Warrior came up on its banks after the heavy rain we'd had the night before.

"Pull over here, baby," he croaked. I did.

"You know Pop used to own all this land around here."

"No, I didn't."

"Well, baby, he did. We lived in a shotgun house over that hill right there while they put a new roof on the Old House. And one day, while he was out plowing, a preacher came to call."

I tried not to smile, pretending he'd suckered me in.

"Momma saw him coming up the road and sent me running out to get Pop. I couldn't have been more than six. I finally got out there huffing and puffing, barefooted and one strap dangling loose on my overalls, hollering 'Daddy, Daddy, the preacher's come calling!'

"'What kind of preacher?' Pop asked me and I shrugged.

"So I asked him, 'What do you mean, what kind?' And Pop whoa-ed the mule.

"He told me, 'Son, you listen up good. You run back to that house and if that man has his collar on backwards, you hide the money can under the bed.'

"I nodded, and Pop went on. 'If he says he's Episcopal, you hide the whiskey under the bed.'

"I told him I would.

"Pop thought about it a minute, then said, 'And son, if he's Methodist, you grab those two potato pies your momma made and you slide them under the bed.'

"I turned and started running, and Pop hollered after me, 'And don't you dare forget: if he's Baptist, you sit in your momma's lap till I get home!'"

A woman sat down next to me on my grandmother's porch swing the day we buried my father. She looked about sixty, in good shape and dressed in a pale blue linen suit with earrings to match. She handed me a glass of tea and a saucer with a square of Mexican cornbread on it. "I made this myself," she said. "You need to eat."

I took a bite. "Your daddy was a fine man. You know, if it weren't for him, I wouldn't have ever got my Cadillac." She pointed to the shiny pink car parked out by the curb, and we reminisced about that day we'd dined on catfish and laughed together over that old joke.

"Daddy never did tell me why he hated Baptists so much. I guess I'll never know now."

She patted my hand, "Honey, your daddy didn't hate Baptists. Your daddy just loved a good story."

I thought about it a minute. "I don't know. He never would let me go to Sunbeams with Elizabeth."

"Darling, he probably just wanted to see you out playing on the swing set when he got home from work. Either that or he didn't want to have to drive over to the church to pick you up. I wouldn't worry about it anymore if I was you."

So I didn't. I watched her drive off as I cleaned my plate. And that woman sent us a check every month till she paid off what money she was still owing.

The Company We Keep

n light green rooms that smelled of pencil shavings, terrariums, and our stiff new shoes, we learned rules and one another's names. We spent most of our first days of school playing Farmer-in-the-Dell, listening to stories, and cleaning up milk we spilled trying to open miniature waxed cartons. Just two months short of seven, I stood a head taller than most other kids in Mrs. Loughborough's first-grade class.

Tuscaloosa had no public kindergartens in 1958, and when I had begged, my mother hushed me up. Nobody went to the private ones, she told me, except a bunch of titty-babies who needed special help before they could go to real school, so I waited another year. I stood tall and ready, enunciating my best when we pledged allegiance. I tried to comfort less-confident classmates and I listened up good, eager to absorb whatever learning might come my way.

We sang in school every day until I finished the sixth grade. Folk songs about Old Dan Tucker. Rounds about fairies in gardens. Our haunting lied of a state song. New ditties about weather and memorable dead presidents. On our first day, Mrs. Loughborough taped eight construction-paper outlines of balloons on the bulletin board. Pointing to the first one, she warbled, "Blue balloon, blue balloon, who will buy my blue balloon?"

Sheila Poole, a chubby towhead whose dress matched the balloon in question, raised her hand. Mrs. Loughborough motioned her to the front, and stood with her hand on Sheila's back. Together they sang, "Blue balloon, blue balloon, I will buy your blue balloon," and our teacher reached into her pocket and gave Sheila a grape Tootsie Roll Pop.

Seeing the reward, my classmates nearly dislocated their shoulders vying to purchase the remaining balloons. The green one fell to the floor and slid under the teacher's desk, dislodged, perhaps, by the breeze our eager hand-waving created. Mrs. Loughborough taped it up again before continuing her musical auction. Finally, only one balloon remained. She pointed and sang, "Brown balloon, brown balloon, who will buy my brown balloon?"

Quiet came over our classroom so quickly we could hear the wall clock ticking. Somewhere outside, a ball went through a rusty chain basket and the water fountain gurgled in the hall. Mrs. Loughborough realized her mistake, but set her chin, embarrassed to admit it. "Brown balloon, brown balloon," she sang out again, louder this time, but nobody bid. A few big boys on the back row snickered.

With only five to seven years under our belts, every last one of us knew better than to subject ourselves to the scorn and ridicule sure to follow the owner of a balloon the color of mud, of dirt, of Nicodemus and Sambo and way, way worse. Not even for a Tootsie Roll Pop. We could not read the words "white" or "colored" either, but we knew to sip from the fountain with the shiniest handle.

My teacher's cheeks reddened up some, and the corner of her mouth twitched a little right where some of her lipstick tended to seep into wrinkles. I could not tell whether she wanted to stomp out of the classroom or rip the brown balloon off the wall or bawl. She might have sent us all to stand in the corners if the room had had more than four.

Her unhappiness hurt me to watch, the way it followed close behind her kindness and her confections. One in front of twenty-six, and us all laughing at her. For some reason I also felt bad for that brown balloon nobody would buy. Holding a cinder block could not have made it harder to raise my hand, but I did. I screwed my eyes up toward the ceiling and sang right out loud, the way I did in church, pretending it did not bother me at all.

Several children laughed at me. Sherry whispered to Nina behind her hand and both giggled. And a blue-eyed boy in a pressed white shirt met my eyes and smiled with a slight nod of his head. Then Kirby smiled bigger, showing lots of gum above his top teeth. A smile too big for his face, but exuding a goodness that rescued me from disgrace.

By the third full day whenever our teacher asked for a volunteer I glanced at my skinny new friend. Kirby's pale blond hair curled loosely over a high forehead. You or me this time, buddy? One of us would square our shoulders. We weren't scared anymore because, hell, I was a year older and Kirby was just damn smart. Sometimes he would raise his hand. Others, Kirby would look at his feet and shake his head, and I would stand. By the time we stayed at school a full day, I knew to save him a seat. "Is that for me?" he asked, holding his Gunsmoke lunchbox in front of his chest with both hands, and I smiled up at him. He thanked me. After that I never ate lunch without him except when he had chicken pox.

Kirby came from money. On his creased trousers, I never saw a patch or those bleached-out lines indicating let-down hems. Nobody had worn his pants before him, so I knew his daddy either taught out at the university or signed my daddy's paycheck at the paper mill.

His lunches looked better than everyone else's too. Certainly better than my thirty-five-cent board of education meat-and-two on the plastic divided plate. My mother dug loose change out of the bottom of her purse as we were running out the door and she often came up a nickel short. Kirby brought thick, crustless chicken salad sandwiches, the wheat bread cut on the diagonal. His frozen orange would thaw to slightly chilled perfection by the time we ate our snacks. Often he brought an extra home-baked brownie for me.

Mrs. Loughborough privately instructed us not to use the term "highest" when referring to the reading group Kirby and I comprised. "Now how do you think that would make the other children feel?" Kirby came in on the first day able to read the golden rule on the wall and I latched onto phonics without breathing hard.

Our teacher told us to choose bird names. Kirby and I named ourselves the Nightingales. Six other children managed to figure out what Dick and Jane were up to pretty fast, and called themselves the Yellowhammers after the Alabama state bird. About half the kids looked up for approval after each stretched-out word, pronouncing all the vowels long. They became the Blue Jays. And the four poor Robins barely knew how to hold their books right side up.

Mid-October the weather turned cool enough for me to wear my new red sweater. I heard my mother talking on the phone when I came home. "Of course," she said, "but only if you call me Margie. Wednesday? I know she'd love that." She spoke in the voice and accent she used with the preacher and her boss. "I can pick her up at 5:30. Yes. Um-hmm. Second entrance. We'll both look forward to it."

"Well, la-di-da! Ar-kay-dee-ah!" she sang, turning to me after hanging up. "Look who's got herself a little boyfriend, and from such a fancy neighborhood, too!" Every time I looked at her that evening she smiled at me like I'd picked her a handful of daisies. Tuesday night she washed my hair, using an extra capful of her Breck creme rinse.

A remarkable painting of a young brunette hung in the foyer of Kirby's home. The subject gazed back over her creamy shoulder in a three-quarter profile, the deep vee back of her evening gown accentuating a tiny waist. "This is my big sister Sarah," Kirby explained, as if she were present for the introduction. "She's off at Sweet Briar." I had never heard of Sweet Briar and I did not want him to know that. It sounded so lovely that I knew all smart people should know about it. I envisioned Sarah sleeping in a faraway castle like the ones in my books, dreaming where bramble-roses grew up wild and hid every brick with their blooms.

Kirby and I ate vanilla ice cream served by Jimmie Nell, then played in his room. He showed me his encyclopedia and I told him about mine. We discovered we both favored volume D for its illustrations of dog breeds and modes of dress through the centuries. We tried to pick favorites, and I could not decide whether I liked bustles best or the shoes of the Italian renaissance, the ones with the toes that curled up around themselves like a pug's tail. Kirby preferred the togas, clasped on the shoulder with Grecian gold. Pharaonic beards came second. I considered the bright pictures in our white leather World Books far superior to those in his burgundy Britannicas, but kept it to myself.

Odd bits and snatches of the afternoon flash through my memory like a fat book thumbed through too fast. His dog played dead on command, I think. Maybe he had a rock collection heavy on mica. Only one thing we did comes into clear focus.

"Can you keep a secret?" Kirby asked.

I nodded.

"Follow me."

"Sssshhhhhh," Kirby warned me, tiptoeing down the long carpeted hallway. He closed the door behind us, slow and silent in the dark. I inhaled layers of a cool deep scent, like my mother's Sunday handkerchief. Kirby listened, making sure his mother had not heard us, then flipped a light switch.

Billows surrounded us, as if we'd entered a pastel cave with puffs of smoke for walls. A mirror covered one wall, reflecting the row of evening gowns suspended on the other. I reached out my skinny tanned hand, half afraid the fabric would soil or rip, but irresistibly driven to memorize the texture of a chiffon the color of sand. Crisp, bright organdies, and these somber and impossibly rich velvets. Overwhelmed by clouds of beauty, I sank onto a lavender cushioned bench.

Kirby shrugged and giggled at my astonishment. He glided from one end of the room to the other, trailing his hand across the luscious fabrics, motioning me to follow. I obeyed, learning this smoothness by heart.

Chewing his lower lip, he looked me up and down, then handed me a blue petticoat with scallops and bows, and helped me fasten it so that it trailed behind me like a cloak. He pulled two large safety pins from his pocket and took down a long yellow petticoat, layers and layers of net, from its padded satin hanger. After draping it around his thin shoulders, he pinned the waistband around his thin neck.

Kirby stepped up onto the bench, struggling a moment to balance in his drapery, and beckoned me up with a lift of his chin. Side by side, we admired ourselves in the mirror, hypnotized. To this day I swear I have never worn anything that made me feel as beautiful.

Bending down, he lifted his hem between his thumbs and forefingers. I did the same. Without a word, we simultaneously raised our arms. Our wings unfurled. With auras of lace from our throats to our ankles, we glided our arms up and down.

Kirby and I did other things together over time. We made up songs about our teachers and played Scrabble. Acted out scenes from the movie *Pollyanna*. We wrote a book together in the fifth grade, a parody of *Jane Eyre* with our principal cast as Brocklehurst. Not once during my elementary school years did I invite another boy to my birthday parties. Only Kirby. He brought me the nicest presents, a big picture puzzle or, later, gorgeous Barbie outfits—the real Mattel ones with accessories. But of all the things we did together, only the closet game stayed secret.

We had no name for it, but we played it often as we could, played it for five more years till we knew we'd grown too big, but we played it still. We signaled our readiness for it without words, with gazes, with significant glittering looks, like lovers watching clocks and waiting for the hour when they can draw the curtain and turn to one another. Alone together we watched our reflections flutter in Sarah's closet, as fragile and forbidden there as moths, until my mother moved me away.

Just about every white family I knew had a maid back then. Rich or piss-poor, it made no difference. Most employers paid them a pittance, paid in cash so they did not have to fool with the IRS. Give them a few bucks a day and send them home toting—carrying leftover food, clothing, or household goods. Social security or minimum wage be damned.

Kirby's housekeeper, Jimmie Nell, was different. She wore a dark gray uniform with a starched white cap instead of our castoffs, and her English sounded good as ours. Better. Never once did I see her swat at Kirby or boss him freely or threatened to romp on his britches. She spoke to him in soft tones, like someone used to both the giving and the receiving ends of respect. And she had a set of keys to Kirby's mother's car.

She took us to Queen City Pool a few times over the summer after the first grade. Kirby and I sat, swimsuit clad, in the back seat of the Lincoln. The moment she parked, we jumped out and ran, lured by chlorine and echoing laughter. Jimmie Nell called us back, needing to hold our hands, not to protect us, but to make clear her reason for entering the pool. She paid two quarters from her apron pocket. No charge for her. Since neither of us could swim, she restricted us to the kiddie pool.

Joyous beneath a pink shell-shaped fountain, we splashed and paddled as Jimmie Nell watched, staying in what little shade she could find, her gray uniform almost invisible next to the bright tropical prints of the mothers. A few times I noticed children watching us from the top of the hill outside the tall chain-link fence, up where the blackberries grew. Children our age or a little older. I never wondered why they couldn't come swim because by the time we turned seven in Tuscaloosa, we all knew why and we knew it rude to mention. Once I did question Jimmie Nell about what they did up there on that ridge.

She was combing and toweling my wet hair so I wouldn't drip all over the car. "Just up there living and getting hot, honey," she told me, rubbing my hair a little harder than she had to. "Just getting too hot is all."

When I was in the sixth grade, my mother woke us up in the middle of the night and moved us across town to a rented house. I told her I did not want to change schools and she told me I had to, that the board of education required it. I later found out this was not true. She made me leave the school where I had been happy for five and a half years, where I had been elected student council vice-president. She did this, I believe, out of hurt. She could not bear the disapproval of neighbors she'd known so many years.

I stared at the telephone for three afternoons in a row before getting up the nerve to call Kirby to explain to him what had happened. I had to call him because I had invited some friends over for ice cream and cake to celebrate my twelfth birthday. I did not want a party any more. I did not want anyone to see this drab white shingled house with the pictureless walls and to know I lived there. I don't remember how I said it, but I know it was the only time in my life I felt my face heat up with shame in a room all by myself. I told him he could not come to my birthday party, that my grandmother would only let me invite girls.

"That's not true," Kirby said. "You don't want me to come because of what happened with your parents. I think you feel bad, maybe about them or your house or something."

"Bye, Kirby," I said, and I hung up the phone, humiliated that he knew the truth and told it.

My mother remarried fast enough to cause a lot of high talk. It hurt her in some deep ways and she never got over that hurt. She yanked us away from people who cared about us and she kept us away. Married a man who was cussing a blue streak whenever he wasn't calling me spoiled rotten or slipping his thick slug of a tongue down my twelve-year-old throat in the hallway while my mother cooked our dinner in our new brick ranch house.

At my new school, the other sixth-graders loved me for three days, as I had the good fortune of starting on the day of a spelling bee.

All the girls scooched over to make room for me in the cafeteria. On the fourth day the rain stopped and we chose teams for kickball. Mrs. Bayne made everybody play. Easy out, easy out. After that, I ate my lunch alone, thinking I'd give up dessert forever, give up anything but my little sister or my collie, to be sitting on the swing with Kirby, or singing with the children I had helped learn to read. Children who loved me in spite of my braces and the way my ears stuck out, who knew me as a kind and tender girl, and who wore the same kind of socks I did.

Rest of the sixth grade I stuck to myself. Not hard, since nobody wanted the desk next to a scrawny country girl who didn't smell like Ambush or know enough to act like she wanted breasts. I never let any of my classmates look at my report card, not wanting them to see my mother's signature, as she insisted on signing with her new name that did not match mine. I did not know any other children whose parents had divorced. When Sally Marrott snatched the envelope out of my hand and asked about the difference in our names, I told her my aunt had signed it because my mother was on a vacation in Greece, and I cried that night, ashamed of my feeble lie that nobody believed.

I taught myself not to think about Kirby too much, the way you teach yourself after a time not to pine over a pet gone missing. Still, you know every day that your life is not as sweet and you feel for the absence. Kirby got lost to me.

I got zoned to Tuscaloosa Junior High the following year and he got zoned to Eastwood. We all had to be new kids then, and whenever he crossed my mind, I remembered Kirby in a once-upon-a-time way. My little childhood buddy. Three years would pass before we'd both attend Tuscaloosa's predominately white high school. By then my braces were off. My teeth glistened like a row of Chiclets, and I had me a new best friend.

Momma dropped me off at my new school during her lunch hour one afternoon in June before I started the seventh grade. I found the room the letter specified and entered the paint-peeled auditorium by myself like it did not bother me a bit. A woman wearing earbobs that read "Roll" on one ear and "Tide" on the other took my letter from my hand and pointed to a chair in the front row. I waited quietly as I could, straightening the hem of my new green floral-print Villager shirtwaist dress—the kind older girls wore. Two months' babysitting money and going without Fruit Stripe gum for one dress and a pair of stockings. No more socks for me. A new chance within my grasp and damned if I'd piss it away. About forty students sat next to one of their parents. One other girl waited alone.

Forty years ago now, and I've still never seen another person who looks anything like Jinkie. You could almost see through her thin white skin. Peach-colored freckles hopscotched across the round of her cheeks and the bridge of her nose. Her dark auburn hair hung straight and lanky. When I see her in my mind, her hair reminds me of those beaded curtains we all strung across our doorless doorways a few years later. Like a sheet only a hair or two thick. Grab one strand and the whole sheet shifts and resettles. A big unapologetic Barbra Streisand nose plopped smack in the middle of her broad round face. Look at her and you could see her wayward courage brewing behind eyes adorned with way more eye makeup than my mother would have let me out of the house in, me with my Tangee Natural lip gloss and Angel Face blush.

Her ankles stopped too thick at the end of her legs and her shoulders started up too narrow for her neck. I could not tell what she had on under her navy blue trench coat, the kind the girls all wanted in 1965, but I knew she hated it because why the hell else would she be buttoned up to here on a Tuscaloosa summer day and not cloud one in the sky? She looked too big-boned and red-headed, too pale and way too proud. Looked like she knew too much to sit with a little girl like me, her with her smart one-sided smirk. She looked like a girl made out of spare parts.

The school secretary called two names—mine and Jennifer Fields. Jinkie and I walked to the front to stand shoulder to shoulder, speaking not a word. A fat man and a skinny man, both with their ugly ties loosened against the heat, approached us. The bony one reached out and started squeezing the corners of my mouth together between his thumb and middle finger and the other took to scribbling on a clipboard. I turned my eyes to the acoustic ceiling to avoid looking at him, my lips forced to suck toward heaven like a guppy's would in a bowl of dirty water. They did the same thing to Jinkie's mouth, then turned their backs on us and began a discussion of what they called our UM-bashures.

Our embouchures pleased representatives of the Alabama Music Educators Association. We made high scores on the music aptitude tests the school system required. Since the shapes of our mouths fit the bill, the county would pay half the cost of any instrument Mr. Smitherman and Mr. Silvio deemed us physically capable of playing. They liked us both for brass.

Mr. Smitherman reached into his pocket and lifted a silver funnel-shaped mouthpiece to my face. He instructed me to press my mouth to it puckered up tight and to force air through without parting my lips. I obeyed, making a fart noise into the silver. It bleated sharp and short through the room like an amplified duck call.

A few boys snickered, then flinched from parental elbows. Mr. Smitherman wiped the mouthpiece on his handkerchief and held it to Jinkie's mouth. She flashed her eyes at me, then met his on the money, and buzzed a long low C-note, then tightened and went up a step to E, squeezed harder but with control and out came a G. Pause for effect. Then, she blasted out a deafening high C, crossing her eyes as she did it.

"My brother plays the tuba," she whispered to me when we sat. "Call me Jinkie. Let's me and you take a walk." She opened her purse so I could see a pack of Chesterfields inside right next to a butane lighter and a pack of Fruit Stripe gum. My favorite, and I figured I could fake it enough with the smokes to not embarrass myself. I'd have followed her into a lion's den and felt safe doing it, strong the way she seemed.

Given our choice of brasses, we chose the French horn for its roundness, its richness, its jovial mellow tone. We began our lessons together that summer, sweltering in the humidity of the Tuscaloosa Junior High School bandroom, learning how to tighten our lips and use the keys for the high notes; how to let them go soft to blow low; and how to triple-tongue—ta-da-kah, ta-da-kah, ta-da-kah—for the parts marked allegro.

After our lessons, we'd bike downtown for ice cream sodas at the Harco drugstore or over to the university campus to sit on a towel on the quad. Someday, I confessed to her, I wanted to become either an archaeologist or a writer. "You'd be good at either one," she told me. "Hell, I don't know what I'll end up being. Something fun," she said, a hint of devil in her eyes before she hunched over, painting the toenails on her left foot lavender and those on her right foot red because she could not make up her mind and the stripes had not worked out the way she had hoped. "Something without a boss. Something you don't have to go to school forever for."

We discovered that we had been born two days apart in December. She showed me a snapshot of Bogie, her fat black and tan dachshund, with a hot dog sticking out of his mouth like a cigar. Lacking supervision or responsibility, we spent our days memorizing one another. We'd ride back home when we heard the Million Dollar Band tuning up for practice.

Once school started, we could not talk as much as we had gotten used to. We started writing notes to each other, letters really, about boys and teachers and our dreams. Who said what. What they wore when they were saying it. What we'd rather be doing than what we were. We signed them with aliases in case of interception or confiscation, stealing our pen names first from cartoon characters, then from Beatles songs.

"Dear Natasha," she would begin. "Martha, My Dear," I would reply. We exchanged notes in the hall on the way to class, squeezing each other's hand as we passed.

The comments we wrote were often cruel, making fun of our classmates and teachers in a way that made me feel ugly and shriveled inside, mean in a way I'd never been mean. Still, I wrote them. Once in a while, I'd recollect Connie Lee's advice. "If you're ashamed to sign your name or get your picture taken, you ain't got no business saying it, writing it, or doing it." And my conscience would catch for a second when I thought about her, her good advice, her constant love, and her absence.

Jinkie stood closer though, stronger, and she burned way brighter. She could drown out Connie Lee without even knowing she had a rival for my soul. That December, Jinkie gave me a typewriter charm for my bracelet. I gave her a little silver dachshund for hers.

I knew Jinkie's father drank. Whose didn't? Hers, however, drank in a way that got him fired from the used car lots where he worked, made her mother threaten and scream and schedule long family prayer sessions with their Wesleyan Methodist minister. Her daddy ended up on the second floor of the Tuscaloosa County courthouse on more than one occasion, making sorry excuses for parking his car in the neighbors' petunia bed. Sometimes I'd see him on the front porch swing when I walked Jinkie home from school. He'd sit swigging from a bag-wrapped bottle of something or other and waving like an idiot, his thin white hair sticking up every which way.

Jinkie either swore in disgust about her father or laughed at his antics. It depended on her mood. Once he started snoring, she'd steal his rum, siphoning it into a rinsed-out Jungle Gardenia perfume bottle. We'd sip it slowly the next day in the girls' bathroom, savoring the floral aftertaste. She'd tell me how he pointed at her with half a right forefinger (he having left the upper digit down to the second knuckle on some World War II battlefield I'd know today if I had not stayed so stoned in high school) and called her a marijuana-smoking poopoo taking the fast track to eternal damnation.

I got invited to Jinkie's house to spend the night one November Friday when her father got hospitalized. This happened more often than you'd think. Jinkie told me his back had seized up on him in a serious manner, but I knew better. My mother 'd been working as the nursing-home secretary over at the VA ever since we moved across town, and she told me he had gone in to get help with either his liver or his drinking. I forget which. I felt sorry for Jinkie, and I acted like I believed her till I did.

That night after we ate the spaghetti dinner her mother had made us, we sat up in her bedroom, knees touching, shoving the planchett back and forth over the Ouija board till we got either bored or scared. Suddenly, Jinkie snatched my hands into hers. I jumped, startled, and she squeezed hard enough to make my fingers ache. "Can I show you something?"

"Sure." I nodded, wide-eyed.

"Promise not to tell?"

I swore with every sacred needle-in-my-eye childhood oath I could muster. And I never did tell till now. I think it's okay to tell now, since nobody much is left to get hurt by the telling.

"Follow me," she told me, beckoning with her left hand. We tiptoed halfway down the stairs, stopping on the landing. She undid a rough wooden painted-over latch, paused, and pushed open a narrow door I had not noticed. We entered, and she closed it behind us without a sound.

I stood in the dark with Jinkie, listening to small scurryings in corners of the chilly space and the sound of her inching forward, then the snap of a pull-chain. I scrunched my eyes shut against an unexpected jolt of light.

Attics all look the same—a muddle of tangled Christmas lights, boxes of camphored-down clothing, a red rocking horse with one spring rusted and the other one busted, and four stacks of disintegrating magazines kept for articles nobody remembered reading. In Jinkie's house, the whole mess rested on unfinished floorboards too old to have splinters. A grownup could stand in the center once they crawled through the entrance. Knob and tube wiring peeked haphazardly out of the gray cotton candy of loose fiberglass insulation. Jinkie took my hand and drew me closer to a trunk with a peeling veneer, long ago shoved into a far dark corner.

Looking old as it did, the lid should have creaked open, but it rose silent and easy, revealing the random embroidered mosaic of a faded crazy quilt, seams splitting here and there, tucked in too carefully at the corners. Jinkie reached beneath it and pulled, unfurling folds of heavy white cotton. I knew what she held from pictures my half-uncle Sonny had shown me, magazine photographs my mother had cursed him for bringing into our home.

Jinkie draped the robe over my shoulders and fastened a loose belt around my waist. The garment had substance and structure. The sleeves trailed down over my hands and the hood fit almost flat on my head, not pointed high the way they did in political cartoons. A biblike square draped across the lower part of my face like a burka's veil, and I turned to a chifforobe's cracked mirror to see my eyes reflected through the slit.

In spite of the garment's weight, the room felt colder to me. I could not read the emotion in my own eyes. It looked like terror at first, but my chest pounded with the exhilarated heartbeat of a child getting away with something dangerous and fun until I thought of what somebody had witnessed through the narrowness of this portal.

I shuddered and took a deep breath in. That's when I caught it, and ever since, that smell is what I remember most. You'd think it might hold the scent of smoke, or an atticky perfume of mouse and mothwing. But it carried the odor of old sweat, folded-up-dirty and stashed-in-a-hurry sweat, and not the kind men shed from any honest work. The robe stunk the way fear stinks, embarrassing, sharp, and sour.

I stripped it off me in a sweep, hugging myself and staring at it on the floor in front of me the way I would at a puddle of vomit. Jinkie lifted it matter-of-factly, folded it, and covered it with that quilt, stitched, perhaps, by the same woman who had fashioned the robe. She looked me dead on and whispered, "He was Klan when we lived in Georgia." People said it that way then. "He was Klan," the way they might say someone was Republican, Baptist, diabetic, or Navy. And that phrase, that way of defining, still makes sense to me. What he belonged to stood in for politics and religion, and once he got inducted, it took him like a sickness would and never did let him go.

Jinkie and I never spoke about the robe again. After leaving the attic we locked ourselves into the upstairs bathroom and sat on the side of a clawfoot tub. I took a whole Chesterfield myself instead of having a puff or two from hers. No filters on those, and bits of tobacco stuck to my glossed lips. We thought we heard her mother's tired step on the landing once, and Jinkie shoved the window up. We sprayed the cool night air with Right Guard deodorant to hide what we were doing, giggling together as we fanned with our open hands. Our little pink-tipped fingers spread like the points of stars.

I'd love to tell you that Kirby and I rekindled our friendship in high school, but too much time had passed us by. He continued his stellar scholastic performance, particularly in Latin, standing in his pinstriped shirt and reciting from Ovid's *Metamorphoses,* making the occasional elegant hand gesture. I made A's in Latin, too, but I got them by goofing off all month, then choking down whatever nameless amphetamine Jinkie had scored at the B&G Truck Stop and memorizing what I needed to know the night before the test. Mrs. Rhodes, our teacher, tried her best to engage me, first during my sophomore year with her chidings about my wasted potential, and later by crowning me with a honeysuckle wreath for my stirring performance as the Queen of Carthage in our Latin Club play, "It's Do or Die for Dido, or Come On, Baby, Light My Pyre." None of this took.

Although he had preceded Jinkie as my first best friend, I never told her. Kirby's pallor and his slight build mattered more in high school than they had when we were children. Some kind of genius, one kid might comment when he passed, and another, just out of

Kirby's earshot, would retort, "Some kind of faggot," and I'd muster all my disdain and hiss, "Shut up, you Neanderthal ass-wipe."

Once in a while I'd see my old friend in study hall talking quietly with Johann Xue, a Dutch-Chinese boy who could do in mathematics what Kirby could do in the dead language. We'd lift a few fingers and smile at each other, careful to avoid the teacher's notice. Kirby probably worried about breaking rules. Usually I was just stoned and did not want to draw attention to myself.

Every year around Christmas, Mrs. Rhodes had all of her students dress in togas and carol through the halls singing in Latin, a ritual we pretended to hate. And I don't mean just "Adeste Fideles." She had chosen her star student to lead us.

As we lined up in rows of five in the hallway, humming and clearing our throats, Louis Colburn, a beef-bodied wrestler who flexed in vain for my attention in algebra, lumbered past. Pausing, he smirked at Kirby. "Looks like he finally found a way to wear a dress to school." The carolers all heard, and so did Kirby. No possible way for him to act like he hadn't.

Kirby's skin flushed, then paled. He stood still, slim as a girl, humiliated but proud enough to try to hide his shame and his fear. Seeing his face (and I can still see it clearly, his trembly expression of trying not to cry), I thought of butterflies, uncertain why that image came to me till I noticed the glittering gilt buckle he'd used to fasten the bedsheet on his left shoulder. I knew he had taken it from the closet where we had spread our lace wings so long ago. I realized this a moment before I realized how those testosterone-glutted athletes, an annoyance to me, menaced Kirby in ways I hated to imagine. Had I been blessed with a speck of talent for ass-kicking, I'd have proceeded with both feet. I couldn't stand to stand still, still I hadn't the strength to make a stand. I did not know what to do till I did it.

I stepped on my sheet's hem, but caught myself before I fell, and stepped up between him and Louis. I smiled my sweetest at the wrestler, then turned to Kirby.

"Sounds like you could use a loud-mouthed alto up here."

"Just about now," Kirby murmured, almost breathless, "you sound like a nightingale to me."

And I hooked my arm in his and began to sing "Tinnitus, tinnitus, semper tinnitus," marching down the long corridor, voices echoing against the lockers. His buckle jingled all the way.

By the time we started high school, I knew I had erred in ever thinking Jinkie strong, but I did not care. Anything could hurt her and did, only she wouldn't let on, and I loved her all the more for this. What she was was fearless, and fearless passes for strong if you don't look too close. She also had a fierce and unquestioning loyalty to me and I needed that so badly those days.

By tenth grade, I had learned not to go to the principal's office when I got called. Most times nothing happened if I ignored the summons. Five hundred people graduated in 1971. The few times Mr. Ingram remembered that he'd sent that note to me and came to get me himself, I got an extra day detention. Often, though, he'd let it slide, so I considered it worth the gamble.

Jinkie and I lit up in the girls' bathroom one morning for a quick visit before first period. Mrs. Robertson, my nemesis, a home ec teacher who hated me for my contempt and for what I did to pancakes, came in just as I had mastered the art of French inhaling. When she told us to follow her, Jinkie sat still on the countertop and I took a step back beside her. The teacher grabbed my wrist, and Jinkie took one more puff, exhaled thoughtfully, then pointed at her with her Chesterfield.

"Woman," she threatened, eyes narrowed, "if you don't get your hands off her and back out of this bathroom this minute, I'll call your husband before lunchtime and tell him about you and her daddy."

A bright flush slid up the teacher's neck. She slapped her hand to her chest. "Doesn't he still work down at B. F. Goodrich?" Jinkie asked.

Mrs. Robertson started backing out, slack-mouthed and slow, shaking her head. Jinkie calmly turned on the cold water and stuck her cigarette under it, then tossed it across the room into the trashcan. "Two points." She smiled at me.

"Holy shit!" I whispered. "Holy fuckin' shit! I never knew about that rat whore and my daddy!"

Jinkie winked and tossed back her hair. "Lucky for you I did."

On days when Jinkie had detention hall, I'd ride my bike over to the university's Amelia Gayle Gorgas Library and look up *incest* in psychology books. What happened to me may not have really qualified, I thought, since it never got bold as rape or even under-the-clothes.

Psychologists say we blame ourselves, feel dirty. I did not. I experienced a sense of sinister enchantment, as if I had chomped into a poisoned apple, swallowed six pomegranate seeds, or pricked my finger on some unexpected spindle and thus had to endure a season in hell. Some nights I awakened to find the ogre sitting on my bed, stroking my hair, then laying his body beside mine and kissing me for a hundred years. I made up my mind that the dire predictions of the experts would not define my life.

I stopped being scared. I could not be scared with Jinkie on my side. I recognized something wrong with the way I lost my fear, though, and I thought about it in the dark before I fell asleep. My anger shot out all over the place with no direction and nailed people who did not deserve it as well as some who probably did.

I regret the way I treated Mrs. Hudson, the menopausal literature teacher who had often praised my expressive reading of poetry. As soon as she distributed our midterm exams, I wrote my name, then scrawled, "I know the answers to all of these questions" lengthwise across the page, folded it, and turned it in. I stared out the window at the parking lot the rest of the hour, avoiding the puzzlement in her eyes.

She called me to her desk after class. I fiddled with my macramé belt as she opened my paper, turning it for me to see. "Melissa" she said, "I know you know these answers. What's wrong, honey? And what am I supposed to do with this?" She began to cry.

It never occurred to me that I could tell her, confess that I had lost Connie Lee, my maiden aunts, my treasures and my neighbors— everything I loved; that I listened instead of sleeping at night; that my mother had abandoned me for a drooling monster and that all my sweetness had taken flight. Instead, I spoke the answers out loud in a sassy rush. Shelley. Yeats. "Ode to a Nightingale." I do not remember what ensued. I only remember sorrow and excitement in my chest, fluttering like a bird against the bars of a cage.

By then, Jinkie and I were doing what they called "experimenting with drugs," although I collected more unexcused absences than data. Nothing scientific about it. Our grades slid on down. We drew the line at cheating on tests, having some sort of thieves' honor, but I had read that on a multiple choice test, B is the most likely answer unless your last option is "All of the above." Always choose "All of the above" if you can. This knowledge usually garnered us at least a C minus.

We bought two blank report cards for two dollars apiece from a friend who worked in the school office. I filled out Jinkie's and she filled out mine every six weeks, sitting on the concrete wall behind the cafeteria as we jotted the letters into the columns. "You made a B this time in Problems of Democracy. How'd I do?" I would ask. "Shoot, you aced that sucker," she'd reply with a wink, then cough out a lungful of ganja smoke. Our parents signed, proud of our progress. We accepted their rewards and forged their signatures on the real reports and never did get caught.

Some of my teachers cared about me, tried to talk to me about choosing my friends more wisely. Tried to ascertain the problem. Others glared at me with "Troublemaker" scratched into their brows. Mrs. Wall, my eleventh-grade homeroom teacher, I knew, would just as soon slap my face as look at me because I refused to pledge allegiance. Every morning after the rest of the kids sat down, she clenched her mouth shut as she glared at me before taking a notebook from her middle desk drawer. Shaking her head, she wrote something in it, then put it back in the drawer.

When Mr. Rinehart called Mrs. Wall across the hall to come sit with his special ed class one morning while he ran to the office, I pounced. To my classmates' titters and gasps, I opened first the drawer, then the notebook.

On the front page, Mrs. Wall had pasted a magazine cutout of the praying hands. Beneath it she had inscribed in poor Gothic calligraphy, "The List of the Lost." Every page contained a list of names and infractions. My own name appeared frequently beside my chief crime: treason. I read a few of the entries to the class, then picked up a Bic and printed in the left column, "Mrs. Wall." In the right, I wrote, "Judging others." I replaced the notebook and took my seat before she returned.

I think we all wanted her to open the book while we were there to witness. When she showed no sign of doing so, Louis Quinn saved the day by goosing Marianne Etheridge. She squealed obligingly. We inhaled as Mrs. Wall reached into her drawer. She opened the notebook to the last page, took pen in hand, then stopped.

Slowly she stood, fisted hands pushing down on her desktop so hard I saw the veins pop up. "Who wrote my name on the List of the Lost?" she bellowed.

To my classmates' credit, none of them ratted me out. The room remained silent as we stared down, fascinated by our desktops, avoiding each other's eyes. I could have gotten away with it had I not been possessed by some demon too strong for a struggle. I smiled at her reddened face and suggested with mock innocence, "Mrs. Wall, do you think it might have been the hand of the Lord?"

I did not mind the five days of detention hall. I did mind the concerned look Kirby gave me, the questions on his face.

By the time we turned fifteen, Jinkie and I needed more than passing notes and the occasional weekend or after-school visit. When we parted after school, I missed her like a junkie misses smack. I'd call her as soon as I got home, talk till somebody started fussing at me to get off the phone. Soon, we started sneaking out of the house. We mapped the shortest route off the main roads, deciding which streets the police weren't as likely to patrol. We left home at midnight, each pedaling a mile in the dark till we met.

Together we headed for the Black Warrior River. We could smell mud and sludge and rotting branches before we saw water. I'd bring a flashlight and we'd drop our bikes in the underbrush and pick our way down through pine and briars, down to where we kept an old tarp hidden. We'd unroll it on the bank, shaking it out before sitting.

On cold nights, we lit a fire and watched it jewel the shallows with its reflection. Once in a while men on passing barges waved at us, mistaking us for hobos. We waved back, smoking whatever we had, sipping what Jinkie had stolen, laughing and scheming and simply being together. At three in the morning we always said goodnight and rode home along empty streets, oblivious to our own vulnerability. My mother woke me up at six thirty on schooldays, my cup of black coffee in her hand, never having noticed my absence.

Before long Jinkie and I started meeting other girls when we snuck out, bad girls, big girls old enough to drive. One summer we spent a lot of time with Theo Santos, a handsome boy from Brazil who drove a Harvester Scout. He looked older, like a grown man. He shaved every morning, judging by the shadow on his chin, and he usually had good pot. He'd take us down by the lake of the country club golf course where we'd get stoned and laugh, watching for the alligator reputed to live in the murk.

Our best nights, our natatorium nights, required some planning. Jinkie lived just two blocks from the university campus. The summer after we turned sixteen, she'd park her bike outside the building in the afternoon while the swim team practiced and slip a folded piece of paper—gum wrappers did the trick nicely—into the side-door lock so the bolt would not slide. Nobody much around at five thirty except the coach and the swimmers, and once she heard splashes and the whistle, she only had to avoid Curtis, a custodian roughly the size of a dumpster, who slammed his mop around with one arm like he was fighting the floor, gnawing on a soggy unlit cigar stub while fingering a roadmap of pink keloid scars on his neck.

Around one in the morning, Jinkie and I would meet at the nat, me panting after the long pedal. The door would open easily for us, noiselessly, and we'd pause for a moment inside, adjusting to the way Bogie's nails clicked tiny echoes across sanitized tile, the way the chlorine scent floated over the undisturbed expanse of water in the dimness of exit lights. Once our senses adjusted, we'd strip, as comfortable naked that summer as not. Each of us grabbed a kickboard and one of us took an extra. Thrilling to the chill of ceramic against our asses, we'd slide into the water, first coaxing the whimpering dachshund to the edge, then cooing to him as we balanced him across the Styrofoam float we held between us.

Mostly we drifted, over our heads, keeping silence other than the occasional sigh or giggle, ferrying Bogie between us till he came to enjoy his dips. We broke in a couple of times a week, and by the end of the summer, the dog stood scratching at the door till we opened it, then waited wagging by the kickboard stack. The three of us floated together, hypnotized by peace, twirling ourselves in the blue so slowly we did not make splashes. My hair dried in the breeze as I bicycled home.

Not once did the danger of what we were doing occur to us until our last nocturnal swim. That night, a low rumbling growl started in

Bogie's throat, building until Jinkie jerked her head around at a click of metal on metal from the side door. Fast as a reflex, she put her hands on our kickboards and shoved Bogie and me toward the side of the pool where I'd piled my shorts and shirt. Bogie slid forward, clawing the water with his stubby legs till I hoisted him back up, kicking frantic and wild.

I pushed him up over the side, his legs running before they touched, his baying ripping the quiet in two as he raced for the door. I slithered for my clothes and slipped three times before I could rise from the wet tile. I looked back for Jinkie, and when I did not see her, my own terror snatched me by the throat too hard for me to scream.

She surfaced on the other side of the pool, the side close to the door she'd jimmied that afternoon. Water rivered down off her hair and skin, glittering her freckled back as she hurled herself up over the side and ran naked toward the noise that had startled us, both of her hands clenched into fists.

She rammed the door open with her shoulder, then bellowed, first in pain, then rage. "You leave us the fuck alone!" Somewhere close by a truck snorted into drive and threw back gravel. "Come back here and I'll kill you, you son-of-a-fuckin'-bitch!"

When I reached Jinkie, she was biting her lower lip, leaning against the door, bent to cradle her foot in her hand. In the moonlight I saw the rosy puff of a quarter-sized blister bursting up on her sole. "Sorry black-assed bastard!" she muttered, staring down to where a cigar stub sputtered at us as lit tobacco sizzled down to saliva-soaked butt. Jinkie coasted home on my bike and I walked beside her. Bogie trotted beside us, pausing now and then to scratch the ground and bluster. I watched Jinkie limp up her back stairs.

During the catharsis of the seventies when we all started facing the truth about our families and telling our secret shames, I realized that during all those nights of escapes and Ouija boards and fireside riverside confessions, Jinkie never once told hers. And I never bothered to ask. This happened way back before made-for-TV movies, before we learned to call evil "dysfunction." Sometimes I wonder about the hobgoblin haunting Jinkie. What made her shiver when she turned out the lights? When she got grown, what kept her going back to the refrigerator for just one more glass? Had someone called her fat?

Stupid? Slapped her around the kitchen? Did the door creak open as she drifted to sleep?

All of the above?

Whatever the problems, they made her cut and run before I did. Right after the first boy she slept with left her, she almost talked me into going too. I snuck out one final time on a May night, saw her standing under a streetlight with a backpack and a cigarette, Bogie on a leash. When she opened her purse and showed me her father's German Luger pistol, I decided. I put down my duffel bag and apologized. I had enough good in my life to make it impossible for me to go, and she had enough bad to make it impossible for her to stay. We hugged goodbye in tears before she hiked toward the highway, her dachshund waddling by her side.

After a month of disappointing stops at the mailbox, I finally got a letter from Jinkie. She had a job in a pet shop in Atlanta, she wrote, and lived with the Outlaws, a very sweet group of bikers who had just gotten a nice write-up in the paper for rescuing a toddler from a burning house they were trying to loot. She enclosed the clipping. Poor Bogie had died two weeks after she left. Kidney failure, the vet said, and she and three bikers buried him in the backyard of the house they shared.

Jinkie saved me that last night we crashed the nat, and not by pushing me away from danger. She taught me what to do about fear. She always ran straight in the direction of trouble and danger, sure as the needle of a compass points true north. When you hear that noise in the dark, whether you waken to crash, creak, thud, or clatter, you have to make up your mind fast what kind of person you want to be: the kind who freezes, who listens again, pulls quilt over chin, and squeaks out desperate prayers, or the kind who rises, darts out to the fray. "You leave me the fuck alone." I practiced the six words. Better, I decided, to grab the lamp, the bookend, the letter opener—something jagged, hard, heavy, and handy. If I lost, I'd fall shrieking the coward's name. If he skulked up on me again, me just lying there, trying to have my little dreams, I'd have something for his ass.

But the six words were all it took. The first time I used them, spitting a little as I hissed them through clenched teeth, my stepfather backed away from me. He narrowed his eyes, nodding a silent threat, a sneer smeared across his face, but he backed off.

My mother looked at me too much the next morning, glanced up too often as she cracked eggs onto Teflon, pitched her voice a little too high when she asked about my lunch money. She had started backing out of the driveway when I saw my stepfather from the front passenger seat of the LeSabre, walking out the kitchen door with an armload of my old dolls we had stored in the attic. Not looking at me, he strode forward and dumped them on top of a pile of white leather-bound encyclopedias on the curb.

My books lay splayed by the garbage can, each volume defiled, its pages crushed and torn. The gold of the titles stamped so deep. The white spines, once strong and straight as a temple's columns. I remembered my hand, a smaller hand from years earlier, sliding volume D back into place on its shelf. Watching the beautiful heap as we drove away toward school, I committed it to my memory. As we passed the well-mown and fertilized lawns, my mother chattered, nervous, weak, and complicit, about the junk we had accumulated over the years. Some stiff doll-bodies sprawled facedown, and others stared up, inert and unquestioning. I did not want them back. The man ruined nearly everything he touched.

I made new friends after Jinkie left, also outsiders but in a different way. Livvie, an actor, had been elected president of the drama club. Annie went to Germany her senior year on a scholarship she earned playing a clarinet. I applied for the feature editor position for *Bear Facts,* my school paper. The announcement of my achievement over the intercom interrupted my Latin class, and Kirby began the applause. I started making good grades for real. I even fell in love for my first two times with a boy named Tom and a girl named May. Another story.

I left home my senior year. I did not run away. I got a minimum-wage job in a shoe store and made arrangements to share an apartment in the student ghetto with Annie, the musician, who had gotten admitted early to the University of Alabama. Then I went home and stood barefoot in the kitchen and told my mother goodbye, told her if she sent after me I'd leave again and again and again till they quit coming for me. And I told her I'd talk out loud about all the things we kept hushed. She sobbed herself breathless at the table and I bucked and left her sitting with a faceful of mascara, door wide open and it pouring down rain.

Must have got herself mixed up with the wrong crowd, the neighbors said. Such a sweet smart child, good grades and sang like an angel in Sunday school. And those curls . . . ! And Jinkie's family probably said similar things.

And they were all dead wrong. Jinkie was no wrong crowd and neither was I. Both of us sirred and ma'amed grownups and trick-or-treated for UNICEF. We were more like two good chemicals that bubbled quietly on our own, but would burn you blind or melt off a layer of your hide if you mixed them together at the wrong temperature. We recognized each other the first time we met, the way you notice someone else who is alone the same time you are. It's just like they're calling to the core of you. Jinkie and I created a wrong crowd of our own.

I shivered down Greensboro Avenue two weeks before I turned twenty-two. Saturday afternoon had been warm for November, and I had left my apartment in a tie-dyed tee-shirt, patched and zodiac-embroidered jeans, and a pair of Dr. Scholl's. Sunday morning I hugged my unsweatered self against the early chill, trying to smooth down goose pimples on my way back home.

Walking past Barbara's Skillet on a Sunday morning took second only to dining there as a way to learn who'd spent Saturday night with whom in Tuscaloosa in 1974. We all tried to go at least once a month just to keep up. Sitting down to breakfast together at this establishment could turn a goodtime hit-and-run into a relationship quicker than registering a china pattern. Cheaper, too, and the lucky couple had the advantage of being able to gorge on biscuits taller than they were wide, so light it took the weight of both butter and honey to keep them on a plate.

As I passed on the sidewalk, I gave the line of people waiting for tables more than a cursory glance, trying to glean a free update, when a group of five men in overcoats stepped out of Barbara's Skillet. One paused to light his pipe. Three headed for the parking lot, waving and calling genteel goodbyes to one another. The last man nodded to the others, fished coins from his pocket, and bent over the newspaper machine on the far end of the porch to buy the *New York Times*.

I watched him slide his paper out from under the one on top. The door of the machine slammed shut. When the man started to straighten his back, he halted sharply. The edge of his coat had caught in the machine's door. He gave a quick tug on the hem, subtle so as not to draw attention to his predicament. When this did not free his coat, he pulled harder, then stopped short quickly, maybe having heard the beginning of a rip.

He reached into his pocket again, counted some change, and mouthed a word I could not hear. He turned toward the parking lot, but his friends had driven away. When he turned back, I recognized Kirby. He looked heavier and older, but then I saw that was mostly tweed and tie. I drew coins from my purse as I cut across the lawn to him.

He had not seen me yet when I reached around him and fed a quarter into the slot. "Oh, dear. Excuse me, please. I seem to have . . ." and then he saw me. He raised his brows and shrugged, gave a crooked grin when I freed his coat and took my *Times*.

Then he hugged me to him, wool scratchy and stiff against my bare arms. "Good heavens, you're freezing!" He began unbuttoning his coat, but I stopped him. "No, no, I'm really fine," I lied, suddenly aware that I smelled like the marriage of jug wine and ashtray in contrast to his subtle aftershave. I raked my fingers through my hair and tried not to breathe on him, him so fresh and me so hungover I felt like I had a dead bird in my mouth. My turn to shrug. "Just out for a stroll and the *Times*."

Kirby smiled almost tenderly at me, pretending to believe me. "I just met some friends from the classics department here for breakfast. Have you ever taken Charles Perry's mythology class?" I shook my head. "Oh, you have not lived! Brilliant man and a delivery like Jack Benny. You'd think he knew the old gods personally."

I smiled. "Maybe I'll take it next semester. I have two electives left. You just home for Thanksgiving?"

Kirby nodded. "Sarah flies in tonight from Baltimore with her husband and the twins. I head back to Bryn Mawr Friday."

"Fast trip."

He nodded. "Too fast, as always. You know, I thought about you last month while going through my old files. Found a copy of *Tragic Days*."

"Gripping, I'm sure." I rolled my eyes.

"Oh, of course," he assured me with mock solemnity. "Indicative of true preadolescent genius." Then smiling again, "So. How is your mother?"

Any number of things could have caused what happened next. For one thing, I'd had way more fun the night before than Alabama law allows. For another, the line outside the restaurant had barely moved, and I noticed people staring at us. Such an unlikely couple we formed, this distinguished young gentleman and that bit of hippy fluff on her way back from God knows where or what, her pupils practically paisley.

Maybe that visible disapproval from the Skillet's clientele got to me. Or it could have been the sudden sharp memory of us as children together, selling our small book, singing our songs, thin voices piping bravely about the wrong balloons. The way we learned words together such a long time ago. I started thinking of the new words we had embraced over the years—mine often coarse or trendy, just short of crude, and his, foreign and ancient. Our vocabularies grown divergent, Babel to one another now.

I suspect though, that I started to cry those great shoulder-shaking sobs simply because so much time had passed since anyone had asked me about my mother or my family or thought of me as a person who had people. I lived alone and I scrambled hard, and once in a while my lack of connection hit me like a fist in the face.

Kirby laid his left hand on my shoulder and offered me an ironed handkerchief. I stared at its whiteness, its narrow blue stripe, and wiped my eyes with my hand instead. "Could I give you a lift home?"

"No, no. God. I'm so sorry. An idiot, really. No, really. The walk will do me good. Clear my head." I knew I could not bear picking my way through the muddy front yard of my rented duplex with him watching, with him seeing my door's ripped screen.

"You're sure?"

"Absolutely. Great to see you, Kirby. Really great. And you call me next time you're coming to Tuscaloosa. We'll have to get together." I walked half a block with the *Times* under my arm, then turned, walking backwards to wave at him. He waved back, smiling. "Oh," he called out, "happy birthday!" Ten years since the last addition to Barbie's wardrobe, but Kirby still remembered.

Jinkie's father lost what he had left of his mind after she'd been gone a few years. My mother and I had forged a tenuous peace by then, and she had told me when Mr. Fields had been admitted to the VA. After living a quiet ward life for a few months, one Friday afternoon he stripped bare-assed naked and stormed down the administrative wing, firing everyone from the director down. He threw open the door of my mother's office and hollered, "You can pack your bags, too, bitch." Everybody laughed around the coffeemaker. Two days later he died.

Jinkie hitchhiked back from Atlanta for the funeral with a wormy black kitten named Razor and a box full of sequined costumes she called breakaways. She had thinned down to sleekness and she had glued a blue spangle to her left temple. I skipped my women's studies class and brewed coffee in an aluminum percolator, trying on her gowns while she sipped and smoked. The costumes weighed so much, heavy with bright beads and glitz, and they stretched down tight over every curve. "Pull here," Jinkie instructed, showing me a concealed tab at the waist. I pulled, and the entire construction fell to the linoleum. We laughed together in my kitchen, Jinkie all in leather and me without a stitch. She did not mention her father, and only shrugged when I asked about the funeral.

She showed me her wedding picture, Jinkie standing alone by a snooker table in a cinder-block-walled living room wearing jeans and a fluffy white veil. Coop, she called the man, short for Cooper. A year later they had separated when she heard him talking with a buddy about how hard it had been to heave some man's body up over the side of a dumpster. Once in a while she thought about moving back home, but Tuscaloosa strip bars could not measure up to Atlanta standards. I dropped her off by the highway on my way to art history.

Jinkie did not go to our thirtieth class reunion, and I can't give you a good reason why I did. I had hated most of those people when they were still young and cute. Mostly I brooded and drank, toying with my old charm bracelet. The Laymen started playing the worst rendition of "Time of the Season" I've heard to this day, and someone behind me asked, "Would you like to dance?" I turned and saw Theo Santos. He told me about his construction company in Atlanta. After high school he had impregnated, married, and divorced the daughter of a local man who had made money by looking at plans for highway development while working as a janitor at the county courthouse, buying up land on the projected route fast and cheap. Never having liked Theo's country of origin, his father-in-law had paid him well to leave the state.

After our dance, Theo and I walked out across the golf course and sat on the grass by the lake. "You know who I saw in Atlanta ten years ago?" He lit a joint and passed it. "Jinkie Fields. Jinkie Cooper I think she called herself." I dropped the joint and coughed as I retrieved it.

"I'd taken some clients to a strip club there. Not a pretty girl, but she always had something and dammit, she still does. Did." I stared out across the lake. "Haven't seen her since," he continued. "You?" I shook my head. I thought I saw something riffling the water across the way. Maybe not. Too far off to tell.

Everybody knows what those vague obituaries mean. No wife, no children mentioned in the clipping my mother sent me in 1993. Die of a four-letter word and that's what you get. The only comforting note mentioned a modest scholarship established in Kirby's name intended to enable promising young classics scholars to study for a summer in Greece. I looked him up in my annual, cried a little to myself. I wrote his parents a nice card, but it came back unopened. Over the years, I almost forgot, the way we do.

In 2004 I stood on the quad at Duke, talking to Richard, a classics professor, about some papyri the library had acquired. He mentioned his upcoming publication on some lofty aspect of Greek sculpture, and it occurred to me to ask, "I wonder if you ever knew my childhood friend Kirby Ellis?"

Richard's mouth went slack and his forehead wrinkled. He shook his head, astonished. "You knew Kirby?"

"We were children together. Best friends back home in Tuscaloosa."

"I just can't believe—I mean, this is so . . . ." he stammered. "You know my partner, Luther?" I nodded. "He and Kirby knew each other at Bryn Mawr."

Richard looked at his watch. "Look, I'll email you. My class starts in ten minutes and I need to collect my thoughts about this." He turned and ran across the quad.

The next day I received the following message:

Kirby died in 1993. He was already noticeably ill when I gave a lecture in the summer of 1990 on the Acropolis to a group of students in Athens. His lecture on the Acropolis Museum and its contents came right after mine. He had no energy then.

After his talk we left the group and went down to the Plaka for a late lunch. He knew he didn't have much time left, and talked about what he hoped to accomplish. I basically listened. I didn't see him again.

I met Luther two years later. He still cried over Kirby's death. He had helped Kirby in Athens, cooking for him (although that became less and less necessary) and cleaning up, and making him presentable when students came to call. They loved him. He was so patient, so brilliant. A sweet, sweet man.

I finally figured out a way to remember Kirby that brings me peace. I envision him resting easy, impervious to viral degradation, in a stucco room with walls the color of vanilla ice cream, breezes and Athenian light filtering through his curtains. His friend has helped, draping him in soft white sheets perfectly arranged to cover his lesions and his frailty. Plump pillows prop him in his bed. When Kirby hears a visitor, he smiles his welcome: the same smile he gave me that time I refused a ride home, only it's a little boy I see, a good little boy waiting for somebody to tuck him in.

Chainsaw racket made it hard to hear the caller. I sat sweltering in a rocking chair up on the balcony at Weymouth Center for the Arts last summer, watching men cleaning up carcasses of felled trees. The number showing on my cell phone not only surprised me, it frightened me a little. My family does not take long-distance lightly, and an Alabama area code often means a family death. Answering, I heard the low voice of Alice, Jinkie's younger sister. Like Jinkie's voice, but without the edge. She had called around Tuscaloosa and finally got my phone number from my Aunt Margaret.

We exchanged the essential courtesies, inquiries about jobs and children, Alice avoiding what she wanted to tell me and me avoiding what I wanted to ask. Finally I mustered, "And Jinkie . . . ?"

"Oh, Melissa," she blurted, sobs choking out the answer. "Jinkie died." I heard a deep inhalation, then a tinkle of ice cubes as a glass hit the receiver on Alice's end. I cannot say that the statement surprised me since I had not heard from Jinkie in thirty years. What surprised me were the catch in my throat and that sting, harsh enough to mute me for a minute.

"Alice, I'm so sorry. I'm so, so sorry. What happened?" I hated to ask her almost as much as I dreaded the knowing. Hers would never be a peacefully-in-her-sleep sort of death. Not at her age. Not Jinkie at any age. The chainsaws stopped for the day, like they were quitting out of respect.

She had died in 1997, died on a Tuesday morning instead of a Saturday night, and Alice still had to have a drink or two to talk about it. Jinkie had left Atlanta and her third husband in the early nineties. Although addicted to prescription drugs, she had been working for the power company ever since, and had advanced to a supervisory position. She lived by herself in a small town in east Alabama. No thunderstorm that day. No other car involved. Maybe the components of some pharmaceutical cocktail she had swallowed didn't sit well together. Maybe she just took a nap. No way to know without enough left to autopsy or even bury, and what the hell did it matter now? The one witness said she simply veered off the highway. Never braked or changed speed, just took a slow turn into a deep gulley, took out a couple of loblolly pines on the way down. She probably died before the explosion.

Whatever Alice had in her glass went down the wrong way. She coughed a few times, then almost whispered, "It's just so goddamn hard to believe, Melissa. She'd been doing good for so damned long."

Neither Kirby nor Jinkie has a grave for me to visit. Friends scattered ashes for both, one on the Acropolis and one into a sluggish Alabama river. Neither had much of an obituary, either. I'm hoping this will serve.

Kirby pointed me one way and Jinkie led me another and I landed somewhere in between. All three of us followed some rules and ignored others. No better or worse than most, I'd argue. He drank fresh-squeezed orange juice every morning and she drank stolen rum in homeroom and I had sips of both.

"There is always one moment in childhood," wrote Graham Greene in *The Power and the Glory*, "when the door opens and lets the future in." He's right. Take your pick. Your father's attic or your sister's closet. Dress yourself however you like: in a hood or in sequins, in a homemade toga or your sister's diaphanous lingerie. Go ahead. No matter what kind of sheet you wrap yourself up in, one day you might do a thing that feels so fine—hell, more than fine—for a minute. Then, because of that act, you might get snatched away. If you're lucky, you won't even feel yourself slip. They're gone and I'm still here, through no virtue or caution of my own. I just got stuck to the world with tighter glue.

A few months ago Livvie called. She told me about a commercial she had made and I told her about my Jinkie and Kirby essay. Sad about Kirby, she said. Such a waste of a brilliant mind. You'd think he would have known better, wouldn't you? She did not remember Jinkie at all.

Lucky I could just hang up the phone. Obscenities boiled up in my mind, all those real obscenities I learned in my teens. I wanted to break full-blown banshee, run through the streets, every stitch of my clothing rent to hell and back, screaming my curses, claws out like a Fury. Call either life a waste to my face and I'll rip out your heart with my teeth if I can, spit it into the Black Warrior River. I'll stuff what's left of you into the nearest dumpster and sleep in heavenly peace all night long. People think they know, but people don't know. Reminds me of what Barbara Graham said at San Quentin just before they opened the gas line and told her to take a deep breath: Good people are always so sure they're right.

Under My Saddle

ention Columbine in 1970 and nothing came to mind but spidery pastel flowers on fragile stems. We did not hear about too many shootings outside of Cambodia or our immediate family. Not that we suffered from any scarcity of firearms. Santy Claus left good little boys twelve-gauge Remingtons. Bad boys got Berettas. Their daddies had them out target shooting before the turkey browned, city limits be damned. Boys learned young how to handle guns and how not to, how guns make messes you can't clean up. Things happened in the public schools now and then, though, that boosted enrollment at the segregated Christian academies that sprouted up like chickweed once the federal government started paying close attention to what color went to school where.

One April afternoon Norris Beatty staggered up from his seat just as the tardy bell started clanging. He stumbled forward, then steadied himself on the teacher's desk. "That girl back there cut me," he whimpered, pulling a red right hand away from his belt buckle.

We could all see that for once in his life, Norris was telling the truth. Not enough blood to drip or gush. More like a slow seep soaking through. You could tell he wasn't done for, although his shirt probably was. Mr. Bennett, our Problems of Democracy teacher, had just entered the classroom. He scanned our faces for an explanation. Finding none, he whipped off his jacket and pressed it against the stain, like if he tried hard enough he could push all that blood back up inside Norris. He put his arm around the boy and hurried him straight out, hollering help all down the hall. You'd think we'd have screamed or cleared out, but we all just sat quiet and looked first at each other, then back to where Cynthia always sat by herself, knowing what girl he meant.

She did not look at us or even look up. She stared down at her desktop, shoulders scrunched and hands in her lap like someone hoping the teacher would not call on her. She licked tears off her top lip and the little white buttons on her blue blouse moved up and down fast and strong enough to notice from the other side of the room. She brought her hands up and gently placed a pocket knife in her pencil trough as if she had just finished some hard test and knew good and well she'd failed it. The tardy bell stopped ringing.

Silent as the room was then, we could hear each of Cynthia's steps tapping on tile when she rose and walked to the open window. She sat down on the sill, stuck her head out, and looked at the ground like she'd dropped a quarter. Spring grass grew thick about six feet below. She had swung one leg over so it dangled outside and was about to draw up the other when Mr. Bennett ran in with the football coach and the principal.

"Don't you do it, missy!" Coach bellowed. Cynthia froze and the three men were on her. They flanked her, grabbed hold, and the skin on her forearms paled from the pressure of their white fingers. Her feet scrambled for the floor but the men moved fast so her toes just dragged. Clear snot and tears tracked and glistened down her face. In the classroom she only made noises on the intake, hissing and sucking gasps. Mr. Kensaw picked up her knife with his handkerchief when they passed her desk. I did hear her start wailing, but way off down the hall. Cynthia left our classroom and our school and she never did come back. After that everyone in our Problems of Democracy class was white.

Some saw it happen but none saw it coming. Norris had this thing he did several times a week. He'd come lumbering in, reeking and sweaty from gym, just before the bell rang when he knew Mr. Bennett would still be smoking in the teachers' lounge. He'd swagger on back to the empty desk next to Cynthia, glance to gauge his audience, give an exaggerated stretch, and plop down, leaning back and crossing his filthy sneakers on her desktop. Some of us shook our heads in disgust, rolled our eyes and murmured idiot or asshole, according to our upbringing. Cynthia never muttered a word, not one word until that

Friday. I guess she just finally made up her mind. She asked him once. "Please move your feet." I saw her say it more than I heard her. Her mouth shaping words she did not have the courage to whisper.

"Whud you say?" His voice carried. Nothing from her, then Norris again, sneering and leaning in. "Whud you say, burrhead?" And that day Cynthia leaned right back, moved fast and silent the way a cornered creature will. She did not swing the blade up, the way you do if you really want to scramble up someone's guts, and she did not slash down like you do to gain force and go deep. Just one quick slit right straight across, shallow enough to hit just knit cotton and belly but deep enough to make everybody pay real good attention to her for that one afternoon.

Thirty-seven years later, I cannot condone that slash, but I can understand it. I remember the incident with guilt, not because I did not grab the knife and not because I never confronted Norris and sure as hell not because I did not tattle. Here's my shame: knowing what Cynthia had to endure, I let that desk next to her sit empty day after day after day. Not five steps away, and me with a heart and two good feet.

Billy Boy

The first man who ever fell in love with me kept real tomatoes lined up on top of the refrigerator all summer long. Organic, maybe, or even what you might call heirloom, but not organic on purpose and not labeled as such. Birds pollinated them, or bugs or breezes. Seeds of these plants produce new generations, but because of the unknown male parent, the tomatoes vary wildly in their characteristics.

To grow them, somebody's grandpa raked up a patch of field and planted seeds he'd put by from seasons past. The family had been growing them forever, just scratching in the seed. They hoped for the best and got it. Nobody living remembered what variety they were and nobody much cared. Country people sat under shade trees in web-woven lawn chairs with bent aluminum frames and sold them in the evening out of cardboard boxes. Fat red sloppy tomatoes with healed splits, still a little bit of green on the stem end. You followed misspelled signs down dirt roads to find them. You could smell vine on them before you cut.

I helped him make tomato sandwiches on days when Shirleen came. He always drove home for his lunch. She'd be ironing there in the kitchen, watching *Dark Shadows* on the countertop TV, the sunlight scented by the beeswax cake she glided over the iron. Plump and dark-skinned, she worked for my mother on Mondays and Wednesdays to pay her Stillman College tuition. A voice major, a beautician had told my mother, a voice people raved about, but I seldom heard her speak, much less sing. Once in a while she'd whisper "Excuse me" when she passed me in the hall. Ironing was her job, not carrying on conversations with a thirteen-year-old white girl, but I would only come home for lunch on days when she was there.

My stepfather took off his boots at the door and washed the chemicals off his hands with dishwashing liquid before choosing the ripest tomato. He peeled and sliced his choice over the sink. Never used a cutting board and never nicked a finger. I'd get out four slices of white bread and set them on two paper towels, slather the bread with mayonnaise, and salt the tomatoes as he sliced. Wordless, we ate our sandwiches together at the kitchen table, ate fast before the juice soaked through, watching that black-and-white vampire stalk the governess.

After we ate, he'd take two sticks of Doublemint gum out of his shirt pocket and offer me one. He'd urge Shirleen to help herself to the leftover tomato slices and if she declined, he insisted. The refrigerator would turn them mushy, I heard him reason as I ran out the door and jumped on my bike. They won't get any better than they are right now. To this day my tomatoes never see the inside of a refrigerator and I won't eat one that has.

In spite of a physique that belied his seventy-five years, my stepfather died this year on a Wednesday night, brought down by a weakness in the heart he inherited from parents he could not remember. His first heart attack, a mild one, tightened up his chest enough to make him call 911 before he fell. When the paramedics arrived, he had to remind my mother of the combination to their burglar alarm. He croaked, "1492," from the living room floor, and then he sailed away and those were the last words he said to her or to anyone else. His second heart attack grazed him a little closer shortly after he reached the cardiac unit, but they defibrillated him right back again. The third one pulled him under too deep to resurface.

"You can always be proud of Billy Linney," my sweet Aunt Mike told me over the phone, trying to ease the sorrow she imagined I was feeling. She had known him since her girlhood. "He left your mother very well provided for and he made every penny of that hisself. Ain't nobody handed that man nothing. He worked hard all his life and accomplished way more than lots of them that come up gnawing on silver spoons. You can always remember that."

I don't look for things to remember about my stepfather. Sandwiches aside. There's gracious plenty I'd as soon forget. When he first married my mother the year I entered sixth grade, I was looking for a lot. He indulged me, teased me, made me sloppy joes. Came home after work every day and asked about my homework like fathers on television, like my own father seldom had. After a few months his attention to me crossed over some line I did not know a name for.

When I balked, he bullied. Soon as I figured out what he was after, I started praying that Billy Linney would die before my mother so that he would not get me the way I knew he wanted to.

He died around midnight. Two days later Memory Chapel Funeral Home buried him. Nothing fancy, everything decided and paid for in advance. He wore his favorite workout clothes, as he had specified in his burial plan. Not a proper funeral to my way of thinking. No visitation, no deviled eggs. His obituary requested donations to the Humane Society in lieu of flowers. Five members of our family and Shelly, my mother's housekeeper, watched a man they had never met crank down the coffin while a Presbyterian minister read a few verses. I could not attend. An unexpected ice storm made it impossible for me to leave North Carolina. When I heard that nobody sang one song, I remembered Shirleen, how she used to iron in silence, never once humming in spite of her glory of a voice.

My stepfather never knew his parents' names. I asked him once, about a decade before he died. He thought his mother's name was Sophia because he remembered trying to say that to call her after calling momma momma mommy so long and it never bringing her back. She had put on her Sunday shoes and handed him a color book but not a single crayon, and set him on the back steps of a ramshackle empty house in the country somewhere outside of Birmingham. "You wait here and don't you move or I'll wear you out," was what she said. "I'll be back soon." And he waited, waited long enough to have to move, but just to pee twice in grass tall as he was, looking over his shoulder although he knew nobody lived nearby. He thought about eating some berries the color of mustard—chinaberries, she'd called them—only she had said not to do that or he'd swell up and die. He sucked his thumb instead, fell asleep sucking.

Finally ladies came for him and took him to the police station. They asked him his name but he never answered. A sergeant past his prime shook his head and sang to himself, "Oh, where have you been, Billy Boy, Billy Boy?" He looked in vain for a pen, then filled out the papers in pencil. "Sheeeeeee's a young thing and cannot leave her motherrrrrr." On the sergeant's whim he became a Billy, never once a William, not even on paper. Four years old or a husky three, they guessed, and he went to the sergeant's home for the night and then to a foster and a foster and another foster and finally two years later on November 9 to the Linneys' farm where he slept in a room off the kitchen and picked whatever was in season after school let out.

A year later the Linneys had a baby of their own. This one grew into a curly-headed miracle of a boy who had a birthday every year. When's my birthday, my future stepfather asked, and they told him to pick one. He picked November 9, thinking this would please them, but they always seemed to forget and he just kept quiet, afraid his reminding might make them mad.

So he came up hard and he came up to labor and he came up lacking in some important ways. He grew cotton and calluses. He picked butter beans and okra, then corn once he could reach high enough. He saw so much out of his reach: money for clothes, money for Coca-Colas with girls after school. Money for college. He learned enough to finish high school, but not enough to live the way people did on *Father Knows Best*. The Linneys gave him their last name and precious little else.

Work was what he learned, and he learned that well. By the time he left his illiterate Cuban first wife and their two children to marry my mother, he had enough money to build himself a house on top of a hill out at North River not a mile from the yacht club. He owned Dixie Pest Control, although he never could get comfortable sitting behind his own desk. Wearing the same khaki uniform as his employees, he drove out to spray houses with them every day. He paid for good financial advice and unlike many he took it. By the time I entered ninth grade, Dixie Pest Control wiped out vermin all over Alabama. My stepfather bought two new cars every year: one a BMW or Mercedes and the other something red to drive my mother to every single game the Crimson Tide played.

Billy Linney never had a close friend. He never belonged to any organization other than his gym and the United States Marine Corps. He did not own one pair of socks in a color besides white. He worked and planned and never asked much from anybody but himself. By 1965 he had a new brick house on the right side of the river, a wife who spoke standard English, and a thirteen-year-old stepdaughter— one who looked like every girl who never had given him a kind word, much less a wink.

In spite of his woeful upbringing, he had to know that what he did to me was nowhere near right. Not too bad, though, I suspect that he assured himself. Not as long as he did not go below the belt or under the clothes. And if I awoke in the night with him sitting on the side of my bed, staring at me like a drunk might look at a locked liquor cabinet, who could prove that anything fermented in his mind beyond paternal affection? And what harm would it do me to stroke my hair just a little, to lie down close enough to inhale a little girlish breath?

Stunned and embarrassed at thirteen, I lay rigid. Unable at first to make myself move my body, I learned to houdini my mind away, to think about my ballet recital or the sock-it-to-me antics of the *Laugh-In* cast. If the moon shone brightly enough, I watched my Siamese fighting fish circling and circling in the bowl on my night table while he finished whatever he did.

After the first few times I got used to it enough to move, and I tried to push my stepfather or wiggle away, but that only seemed to interest him in ways I did not understand. Soon, I could not sleep because if I closed my eyes, the doorknob might turn without me having a minute to brace myself.

I tried telling a few people. I made my art teacher promise not to tell a soul. Unfortunately, she proved a woman of her word. In 1966 nobody made TV movies about sexual abuse and people did not know exactly what to do. I told my father's wife. I think he was breaking in number four that year. "WhatEVER you do, Melissa," she advised me, leaning in so close she nearly spilled her CC and 7, "don't you dare tell your daddy! He'd go shoot him in a heartbeat and you and me'd be driving down to Atmore to take him potato salad on visiting days." Finally, I told my mother.

"You little liar," she hissed. "You have to ruin everything, don't you? You just hate him. Never could stand to see me happy." She stood up from where she sat in his favorite spot on my bed and stalked out of my room. She and I never spoke of this again for over twenty-five years.

I learned to avoid being alone with him. Tricky, because as I got older, his actions grew bolder. He seldom passed me in the hall without pushing me against the wall, grabbing my chin in his hand and kissing me until I could not breathe. He would laugh at the way I panted when he released me, probably envisioning arousal when all I desired was a dry mouth and a lungful of clean air.

My friend Jinkie's balls-out bravado saved me. The "leave me the fuck alone" incantation she flung at anyone who crossed her changed me from victim to viper, and Jinkie never even knew. Even though it put an end to his groping, I found myself unable to swallow a thing sitting at his table anymore, not even with a plateful of pork chops in front of me. My rage at my mother's disbelief choked me to madness, the two of them sitting there like I'd never been hurt. At five foot seven, I weighed 102 pounds. I left that house in 1970. Seventeen years old and I never did go back.

I found a job matching jumbled oxfords in a discount shoe department, then one in a craft store teaching grandmothers how to decoupage the lids of purses shaped like picnic baskets. After two years I realized that neither provided job satisfaction or a living wage. I hightailed back across town and enrolled at the University of Alabama, winging it on federally insured loans and a scholarship or two. Nights, I served up cocktails and a little cleavage to businessmen at Bachelors Three. I seldom saw my kin, although they lived in the same town.

For fifty dollars a month, I slept soundly in a single bed in Ivy Terrace, a decrepit antebellum home divided into six apartments. The circles under my eyes faded. My room had sixteen-foot ceilings, hundred-year-old English cabbage-rose wallpaper, a working fireplace, a redwood picnic table for a desk, and a combination lock I moved from the outside hasp to the inside hasp when I came home. I adopted a six-toed cat, named her Garbo, and taught her to sit on command. I bought pot from an Italian graduate student who'd go door to door every other week with a Wonder Bread bag full of decent homegrown. I'd hand him a five and a ten and he'd grin and hold the bag open. Fifteen dollars bought as much as one hand could grab.

I gained twelve pounds and quit biting my nails. I learned to throw a pot on a kickwheel. I auditioned for and played a part in a university theater musical review. I could recognize several constellations on a clear night and speak basic German with a believable accent. I shared the front porch and the kitchen with three other students, an alcoholic mailman who looked like Harry Dean Stanton before Harry Dean Stanton did, a divorced Avon lady, and a semiretired gas station mechanic who would slap an inspection sticker on your car for five dollars if it passed and ten dollars if it didn't.

Two of the other students and I took Dr. Jacobs's Shakespeare class together one summer. Every Wednesday night we'd each take a part, sometimes joined by Dick the postman. We'd lounge on beanbags, drink cheap scotch, and read a tragedy out loud. Sunday afternoons we'd set up a table on the veranda and play bid whist, sipping Annie Green Springs and inhaling fat joints and the perfume from a wisteria vine over a hundred years old and thick as my ankle.

I had little time and less inclination for housework or laundry. I would wait till all my clothes practically walked around the room by themselves before taking them down to the laundromat on University Boulevard. I crammed the battered machine as full as I could to get everything in one load. Lingering to sniff the steamy bleach held no appeal. Once I stuffed the washer, I'd browse the bookstore down the street. I'd return to transfer everything to one of the working dryers. After wadding my clean hot laundry into a drawstring bag, I'd tote it all back home. After a day or two I might hang or fold everything if I got around to it. If I didn't, I learned, most wrinkles fall out, given time.

One afternoon I went back to retrieve my clothes and found my dryer empty. I searched the graffiti-carved folding tables, hoping that someone in a hurry had simply needed my machine. My clothes were gone. My heart hit the floor.

I had lost every stitch I owned, although it won't sound like I lost much. Two pairs of patched-up jeans, one with a unicorn hand-embroidered on the ass. My mother's old bowling shirt. A nearly new pair of glitter socks. A tie-dyed thermal top. One patchwork skirt. A treasured peasant blouse a friend had brought from Germany. A blue cotton sweater, wrist raveled badly. A once-burgundy sweatshirt faded down to pink. And my only coat, a denim jacket lined with red flannel and here it was November. I hated so much to ask for help that I waited till the next morning to call my mother.

"Oh, Melissa, you are so scatterbrained I don't know how you even . . . ," she scolded. "Why the hell didn't you stay there and . . . ? And what do you expect, living down there the way you do with all those goddamn hippies and heathens and half-breeds and God-knows-what-else and trusting any fool who comes meandering . . . ?"

"Momma, I don't need a lecture," I interrupted, shivering in our unheated hallway. "What I need right now is a coat. Do you want to help me or not?"

"Oh, Melissa, I just don't know how you get yourself . . ." She never could finish a sentence when exasperated. "Oh, I'll call you . . ." Before her receiver hit the cradle, I heard her complaining, "Well, you won't believe what my *brilliant* daughter has gone and . . ." Then the dial tone's hum.

My stepfather called me an hour and a half later. He and my father sounded a lot alike on the phone, and neither of them called very often. When he said, "This is your daddy," it took me a minute to figure out which was calling.

"Your momma told me what happened. Probably niggers."

"Could have been anyone," I said. I did not want to agree and I could not afford to argue.

"Well, I reckon we better go get you something to wear. I'll pick you up at five."

From the wide front porch, I could see his truck a block away, a white Ford with "I'll die for Dixie" emblazoned on the side under the Dixie Pest Control logo, a dead bug with his legs in the air and X's for eyes. He reached across the front seat and pushed the door open. I placed a marker in my library copy of *Le Rouge et le noir* and left it on the porch swing, grateful that all of my housemates worked afternoons except Dick the postman. He had knocked out his deliveries early and was out on the back balcony easing on into his afternoon buzz.

My stepfather bypassed the cheaper shops in downtown Tuscaloosa and took Highway 82 toward McFarland Mall. We didn't have a lot to say to one another. We never had. He cleared his throat a few times like a boy on his first date and asked, "How you doin' in school?"

"Fine," I answered. "Everything's just fine except my clothes."

"Well, let's see if I can help you out some."

I flipped on the radio, leaned back and looked out the window. Sometimes people I've told about him express shock that it never scared me to be alone with my stepfather after I left home, but it didn't. I knew that while he might push himself on a young girl, he needed her fear to find his own courage. I read great literature now, books in languages he could not understand. Ate unsalted butter instead of Blue Bonnet.

Pickings were slim when it came to shopping in Tuscaloosa. My stepfather found a parking place near Gayfers, the town's best department store. Billows of air, Christmas-scented with cedar and cinnamon potpourri, embraced me when he held the door open. I entered without looking at him.

"I'm goin' on down to Sears to price some lawnmowers," he called to my back. "You find whatever you want."

After living on my own for two years, I had forgotten how to want much. Choosing what I needed came easier to me, so I focused on that. I headed for the circular sales racks where jumbled clothes dangled off their hangers. The numbered white plastic dividers bore no relationship to the sizes of the garments. Before heading for the final markdown tables I threw a few things that looked as if they might fit over my arm. I ended up with two pairs of jeans, a pair of painter's pants, and boys' flannel pajamas. A couple of denim work shirts. One plastic package containing three pairs of cotton bikini panties (pink, yellow, and a multicolored floral) and another containing three-for-five-dollars socks.

Billy Linney chose his mower faster than I thought he would. I looked up from the pile of clothes I had selected. He had not seen me standing behind the mirrored column.

My stepfather shifted his weight from one leg to the other, glancing down at his watch. Straddling an invisible line between Ladies' Wear and Cosmetics, he held his cap in both hands. When a red-headed customer reaching for a White Shoulders tester bumped him lightly with her shoulder bag, he leapt to the side as if she had jabbed him with a cattle prod. He dropped his cap, excusing himself and apologizing as he retrieved it. He stepped to the left, teetering a mannequin in a London Fog trench coat. Reeling a little as if the scent from the perfume display intoxicated him, he dusted his cap and rubbed his palm over his four-dollar crew cut.

I took pity and waved for his attention. My stepfather surveyed the drab pile I had accumulated by the register. Thumbing through the packaging the way he would a phone book, he furrowed his brow, then walked away toward the door where we had entered.

Maybe I had chosen too much, I worried. I put back one of the work shirts and pulled the pastel panties to swap them for white. When I turned, I saw my stepfather striding toward me, his jaw set.

He extended his left arm to me. Over it, he carried a golden brown wool blazer. I lifted the hanger, and found a moss green cashmere sweater draped under it, so finely knit you could almost pull it through a wedding ring. In his hand he held a pair of tailored trousers in a green and butternut tweed. His ability to match the colors and styles so skillfully amazed me as much as his generosity until I looked toward the entrance and saw the display in the center aisle. "Fall's Finest," the sign read. My stepfather had brought me the outfit the mannequin wore.

"It's gone be December in a week or two," he explained. "Why don't you go on and get you something with a little warmth to it?"

The price tag on that coat or the color of that sweater—neither influenced my decision to work at forgiving him. The way his rough skin caught on the cashmere, his borrowed name machine-stitched over his pocket—these inspired pity but not mercy. I forgave my stepfather because of his suggestion that I deserved better than the bargain bin, that after all that ugliness I could ask for the best and expect to receive it. That, and his discomfort, the length he went to to piece together something of worth for me. I never did say it out loud.

Three months later in the A&P I saw a woman wearing my German blouse. She was pushing a buggy filled with Little Debbies, Noodle Roni, and a squalling two-year-old dotted with impetigo. It had to be my blouse. The woman looked as if she lacked the sense to cross the street, let alone the Atlantic Ocean. Poor baby probably wouldn't know food for food unless it came wrapped in cellophane. Of course I could not say a word to her, as not a decade had passed since the Selma march, but I hated that woman, and not for stealing my clothes. I hated her for lending credence to my stepfather's speculation.

Thirty years have passed since I lost my laundry. I thought about my stepfather today because tomatoes are coming into season. Heirlooms, the old ones. The heft of them in my hand, weighted like a breast full of milk. That one so heavy for the size of it. This one, cleft deeply into two fat lobes, so like a heart it almost beats in my hand. Who knows what their names are, what they used to be?

Everybody and their sister has written a self-help book for abused girls and I bet I've slogged through most of them. I've done the therapy, the confrontations, the survivor groups where we wore our violations like sad little name tags. The healing rituals, holding hands to take back our nights.

Enough. You can *have* the nights. Granted, I suffered some wrongs as a girl. Once upon a time a pathetic man scared me with his ugly bedtime story. I will never deny this experience, but I refuse to grant it more than its due weight. We all have wonderful and horrible experiences having nothing to do with our own actions, right? Don't tell me you never slid by with a warning when you deserved the speeding ticket. Fifty-five, my ass. You enjoyed that cocktail sent by the admirer who never even oozed up to ask if the empty seat was taken. You've cheated on a test or a lover or a 1040 and dusted your palms and walked, maybe laughed about it later. We don't always deserve what we get. Most times that's a blessing.

Reap what you sow? I'm not buying it. I do value what I learned in Sunday school about forgiveness. Seventy times seven, Matthew wrote. Four hundred ninety times. I usually lose count by five or six. Preachers will tell you that's what he had in mind.

My grandmother backed up those lessons with her admonitions every time I told on my brother. Unable to abide a tattletale, she'd fuss at me out the kitchen window. "Don't you know," she'd holler, forefinger keeping the rhythm on the screen, "don't you know the Bible tells you you'd better forgive and forget or else?"

Forgiveness comes easy to me, the way it does to those of us who grew up loving people with extremely visible shortcomings. I can forgive as many times as I need to. Cut people some slack or you end up snakebit crazy with the poison of the things they'll do. I confess that I falter over my forgetting.

And no damn wonder. Here's another thing I learned in college: Grandma blundered her source. Nobody in the Bible ever once advised us to forgive and forget. Shakespeare came up with that. A mortal man.

We read it out loud one Wednesday night back in Ivy Terrace. "Pray you now," a troubled old man pleaded with his daughter. "Forget and forgive. I am old and foolish." Dick the postman slurred the line a little, it being act four. He'd gone and taken drunk before suppertime, but he got the words out clear enough. He poured himself another shot, proud that his King Lear could move a girl to tears, and him not even a college boy.

Baptism

I n the place where I grew up, children got baptized. They might get beaten with belts and sticks, too, or neglected, or abused in more imaginative ways, but they were damn sure washed in the blood of the lamb to keep the devil from catching hold. And my mother, in spite of her sultry looks, played the piano like an angel, played for whatever church paid best at the time. My religious upbringing was thus eclectic and nondenominational. I was the most frequently baptized child in the state of Alabama. The devil did not stand a chance.

They'd baptize you every which way if you didn't watch out. The Episcopalians poured the holy water down over your head, like Connie Lee washing my hair in the kitchen sink, while the priest, with his embroidery, chanted poetry at you. The Methodists just patted you on the head with a damp hand and then sang those minor-keyed shape-note hymns that would haunt you the rest of your life, assuring you that though your sins be as scarlet, they would be as wool, as snow. The Baptists, lacking poetry, embroidery, or the prettiest music, resorted to drowning the devil and bringing you up dripping and sputtering in clinging robes in front of the gaping multitudes.

If I'd had to pick the one that felt as if it might have worked, I'd go with the Methodists and their hymns. Momma had me onstage, curls bouncing, me singing and dancing without an ounce of stage fright, by the time I was four. Sunday mornings I'd be singing "His Eye Is on the Sparrow," hands folded as if in prayer, eyes on the top pane of the stained glass window the way Momma showed me. In my ballet school's Christmas production of the *Nutcracker,* I danced the role of the Sugarplum Fairy, more by virtue of my curls than my talent. Wednesday afternoons I'd belt out "Chantilly Lace" for Momma's bridge club, the oddness of a nine-year-old in her Brownie uniform singing about spending all her money on big-eyed girls apparently escaping everyone. Momma's favorite was my stirring rendition of "Kiss of Fire," a languid and masochistic tango, the high point of which was me throwing back my head and bringing the back of my hand to my forehead, moaning, "If I'm your slave, then it's your slave I want to be!"

About twice a year, Momma would call Connie Lee and tell her to have me bathed and dressed early, that we were going to visit the Lattners. Daddy and Fred and Momma and Laurette would play poker—Daddy's game, five-card stud, one-eyed jacks wild. No pussy draw games for my daddy. I would be overjoyed at the prospect of these nights, at the excitement of staying up late, petting another child's dogs, eating their candy, and especially seeing my third cousin Nan.

Of course I was old enough to bathe myself, and by telling Connie Lee to bathe me, Momma meant for her to make me take a bath. Connie, however, would take her literally, pretending to run the water the way I told her I wanted it, with all the hot water on one side and all the cold on the other. She'd pour in Cinderella Soaky for bubbles, and tell me to wash my pocketbook first. A lady, according to Connie Lee, always washed the sugar bowl before she even washed her face.

Of all the terms I heard used for parts of my childish anatomy, Connie Lee's were the best. Much better than my aunt's clinical "vagina" or my mother's embarrassed "down there" or my brother's mean-spirited "twat" or the even more Anglo-Saxon terminology used by my father's friends when they were passing bottles and telling jokes. Connie would tickle my ninnie-pies, powder my hineycakes, and I grew up thinking of my body as rich and sweet, all cakes and pies and purses and sugarplums. I would throw myself into my daddy's arms when he came home, and he would bury his scratchy cheek into my neck, calling me scrumptious, come to your daddy, honey, lord, don't you smell good enough to eat!

My cousin Nan, two years older than I, would never have condescended to be friends with a third-grader at school. She had shining black curls, green eyes like all the Delbridges, and that summer, the beginnings of breasts. Once she had let me see them, one night when the poker game had gone on for four hours and Shell was asleep on the floor and the boys were throwing cards into a cowboy hat and we had already been swatted by Callie the maid and threatened twice for jumping on the bed. Few things could enrage my father more than me messing up the bed in a house we were visiting.

"What do you think?" Nan asked proudly, pulling up her pajama top and turning to examine the little swellings from different angles in front of the dressing-table mirror. "I think they're coming along nicely."

"I like them fine. They look real pretty," I replied, embarrassed at having nothing to offer her in return.

"I'll tell you a secret," she said. "Callie told me how to make them grow. If you want them to get big, you have to eat lots of turnip greens."

"You're just joking!"

"No," she replied, her eyes big. "Really! She said that's what all the colored girls do, and look at them!"

I don't know if my family noticed my sudden craving for this particular vegetable. Lord knows turnip greens were plentiful in Alabama. We had them fresh from the patch behind the big house. I ate them almost every day, even drank the pot liquor out of a teacup, and watched. And waited.

Before the summer was out, my daddy had a falling out with Fred Lattner over some business at Fred's cotton gin and the games stopped. We grew older, and I heard that Nan went to County High while we lived in the city limits. I did not see her anymore for years, but I would follow announcements of her accomplishments in the *Tuscaloosa News*. I wondered if she followed mine. I got scholarships, made Phi Beta Kappa, starred in community theater productions, and modeled clothing for local department stores. She made honor society, pledged Tri-Delt, got engaged a few times, and got married twice, the first time for three months and the last time to Mose Tyler, a big sweet rich man who traveled a lot.

I knew this because by the time Nan married Mose, I was a senior at the University of Alabama, working as a cocktail bunny at Joe Namath's restaurant and nightclub, Bachelors Three. I'd dip to serve Mose his martini, and he'd smile and tip well.

For extra money, I did genealogical research for people who wanted to find lost ancestors who'd messed up and died a long time ago in Tuscaloosa County. Every Southern family has its maiden aunt

genealogist, and since I exhibited no leanings toward matrimony, I
was being groomed by my Aunt Linda to record our history for future generations, should any of us feel the inclination to breed.

It was at a meeting of the Tuscaloosa County Genealogical Society
that I learned of the existence of one of my family's ancestral Bibles.
Seems it was in the possession of Nan Tyler, nee Lattner. I called her
the next day.

"Hello, Nan? Melissa Delbridge here. I'm not sure if you remember me . . ."

"Why of course I do! We were all so proud to hear you made Phi
Beta Kappa. Vicki Forest keeps us updated, too."

I could imagine the nature of Vicki's updates. She was one of my
exes, and not known for her discretion.

"Well, I see Mose at Joe's now and then. He'll always kiss my cheek
and we laugh about us being cousins by marriage."

"Sounds like Mose. How's your momma and your Maw-Maw?"

"Oh, fine. Momma's still mean as a snake and Maw-Maw's still in
the Old House, what's left of it. Listen, Nan, the reason I called is
to see if I could stop by one day and look at the Lattner Bible. Ella
Burkhalter says it's full of who begat who in Tuscaloosa County."

"Oh, yes, sugar, it goes back to about 1819, I think—the year Alabama became a state. It's unusual in that it has a list of slave deaths,
too. Some of Callie's people are in it. You know she's still with me."

"You're kidding!"

"No, honey. I'm serious. Her people have been with ours forever.
She's doing great, too. She doesn't do much now but iron and watch
her stories and keep me company, but she gets around pretty good
and helps me out here and there in little ways. I don't know what I'd
do without her!"

"That's great. I know how much she must mean to you."

"You know, her husband Willis is a foreman down at Mose's gin.
They're planning a big retirement party for him next year. Listen, I
could talk all day, but I know you're busy. Why don't you come by
Thursday afternoon around two o'clock? We'll have a drink and chat.
And bring your swimsuit."

I arrived at Nan's ten minutes late on Thursday. Her driveway was
lined in daylilies in full bloom. I parked in the shade of a mimosa tree

and as I closed the car door, she walked around the corner of the house in a black two-piece. I had heard that my cousin had grown into a wild-assed Alabama beauty, and what I had heard was true.

When she hugged me, I smelled coconut oil and gin and sunshine. We agreed that it had been too long, and I followed her into the house. The Bible, binding ragged but pages intact, was laid on the kitchen table on a swatch of velvet. I perused the pages, taking notes on my ancestors while Nan poured the tonic and cut limes. The names seemed to roughen, harden as my great-greats trekked down from Virginia to Alabama, just as their lives had. Miss Lucretia Leftwich married a carpenter, and by the time she died was called Kit Ramsay. Josephine Spicer drowned herself in a well and was buried as Josie Stone near her husband and nine of her seventeen children, seven of whom predeceased her. Later, I learned that my grandmother remembered that drowning. She was only seven at the time. When I asked her why she figured Aunt Josie had done such a terrible thing, she shook her head and said, "Sugar, I reckon she was just plum wore out."

Callie's people appeared on a separate list, recorded with first names, occupations, and sometimes the name of a spouse. Jaybo's Caldonia, laundress. Wealthy's Marvel, driver. Sully, hand. Lucious, hand. Buck, hand.

Nan handed me the cocktail. She suggested that we go for a swim, and took me back to her room to change.

Her room was cool, the walls a darker green than was usually used at that time and in that place. She sat down on the edge of her bed. I could see the lap pool, blue through the gauzy under-curtains of the picture window.

"You see Vicki much anymore?" she asked as I unbuttoned my linen shirt.

"Oh, every now and then. Not so much."

Nan laughed. "Well, forgive me for saying so, cousin, but it looks to me like you've been eating your turnip greens." I began to laugh, and to my surprise, Nan reached up and pulled me down to kiss her, her hand simultaneously slipping down my back to perform a well-practiced two-fingered clasp flick. My cousin Nan neither fumbled nor faltered, unhooking my bra like an expert. I should add that when it is correctly executed, I find this move irresistible, as it reassures me that I am in capable hands.

In case the ease of this friendly gesture surprises you, I should explain at this point that in the early 1970s, there was a whole lot of high-level gourmet screwing around going on in the heart of Dixie. Some of it was even multicultural in nature, although we did not discuss that openly. For situations where the cast of characters got too long to follow without a program, we had competent divorce lawyers who could help us all switch partners and start afresh. Our brothers had not yet brought the four- to six-letter viral sexually transmitted diseases back from overseas. We had a doctor in town, legally licensed if not making medical history, whose name every woman on the high side of fifteen knew. He had created a fine career for himself by building both a discreet parking lot behind his building and a reputation for keeping his mouth shut. Any bacterial or fetal inconvenience resulting from our shenanigans could be taken care of long before Roe met Wade.

I looked at Nan's green eyes, so much like my own, then at her mouth. She had a way of looking you in the eye with her lips slightly parted, as if she were completely enchanted by what she saw. My cousin Nan had a mouth that made you start thinking about things you'd never thought about before, one that made you want to start at one corner and work your way across. Before I knew it, I had started on the left.

People from other regions make much of Southerners sleeping with their cousins, about us going to family reunions to pick up girls. What they don't think about is that since most of us in a town the size of Tuscaloosa are kin to one another if you flip back a few generations, there's really no way to avoid it unless you want to drive up to Birmingham every time you get the urge. You can't swing a cat without hitting a cousin.

Our critics must be onto something, because, truth be told, I did not think twice about Nan. I might have if she'd been my first cousin, or even my second. She was, however, my third, and it wasn't like we were going to make idiot monster babies. They can criticize me if they want to. Their cousins probably don't look like mine. I confess that there were several other occasions that summer when she and I found it necessary to review a few of the finer points of our common genealogy.

Later that afternoon my heart hit the floor at a knock on the bedroom door. To my surprise, Nan calmly called out, "Come on in."

Callie stood in the doorway, tall as I remembered her, hair gone white, completely unruffled at the sight of a well-tossed blond in her employer's bed. "Willis just called from the gin. Mr. Mose on the way home."

Nan smiled gratefully at her. "Thank you, Callie. Would you mind fixing us another gin and tonic?"

"Fresh glasses, baby, or you want me to use these?"

"Let's have fresh ones."

"Yes, ma'am."

We slipped into our bathing suits. The sun was much lower now, so that part of the concrete was cool under our feet, and crickets were coming out. We had our drinks out by the pool, and by the time we heard Mose's car in the driveway, Callie had smoothed out the sheets so I wouldn't get in trouble for messing up someone else's bed. My cousin and I laughed and dove into the water to wash away the guilty stains, the fragrance, every trace of our sins and all that sugar.

Years later, my cousin Jim told me Mose finally ran off with some high-boned blonde by the name of Minunnie Meadows who was reputed to have Cherokee blood. Whether he did this driven by his own passions or because of my cousin Nan's carryings-on was never made clear to me.

Body of Knowledge . . . .

We had all heard rumors, but Alleen Sommers had actually seen it done. By human beings. I'd watched dogs a time or two, and once a registered Charolais bull and cow, so I thought I had the mechanics of it figured out. Still, I gathered with the other fourth-graders by the monkey bars, awaiting enlightenment.

My neighbor Alleen stood in the center, square, short, and so solid you couldn't knock her over with a bat. Red hair sticking up every which way. She had a habit of balling her hands into fists when they weren't busy, like she stayed ready to fight or haul ass if need be, and she balled them now. Her daddy took drunk more than reason or Alabama state law allowed and her mother stayed worn out from taking in sewing and cleaning up whatever her husband dropped, spilled, or puked on. Neither one took time to whisper in front of the kids the way most parents did. They'd holler right in front of Alleen. Consequently, she knew a lot of grown-up stuff that we did not, and her enthusiasm for telling what she learned earned her considerable popularity in spite of raggedy-assed clothes and never a bite of candy to share.

"Okay," she said, eyes making sure we all paid attention. "I woke me last night and I had to pee real bad, so I got up and saw Daddy'd left the TV on and it had done gone all gray and buzzy. I was gonna turn it off and that's when I saw 'em."

Alleen paused and held out a hand. Kenny handed her a grape Pixy Stix and she continued.

"I was right there by the couch and I looked down and there they were, doing sex in the living room!" She looked back over her shoulder, then made us wait while she tore the tip off the paper stick and let a mouthful of purple sugar dissolve enough to swallow.

"Well, how'd it look?" I asked.

Alleen shrugged. "I don't know. Like he was lying on top of her bare-assed and wiggling around and breathing like he'd been out mowing the lawn. And she was lying on her belly underneath him, moaning and carrying on with her titty hanging down over the sofa cushion."

Alleen never failed to impress me. I'd never seen a titty big enough to hang anywhere. I kept trying to get it out of my mind and as soon as it left, up it popped again. I don't think I ever managed eye contact with Mrs. Sommers after that day, not even when she knelt down to put the hem in my Easter dress.

Alleen emptied the rest of the sugar onto her tongue. "What happened then?" one of us asked and the rest nodded. Alleen wadded up her empty straw.

"Okay. I watched 'em till my daddy rared back his head and saw me and he jumped up so fast he knocked over the lamp and it busted all over the floor and my momma fell off the sofa and ran off to the bathroom cussing and now cain't none of us walk in the living room barefooted till the vacuum cleaner gets fixed. Lot of fuss about nothing. Not much to it from what I saw."

But Alleen's adventure got me thinking. Just about every Sunday afternoon my own parents would give us a handful of pocket change and send us down to the corner store to buy Cheetos and Pepsis and what have you. I started adding up those quarters and dimes and coming up with a new theory as to why we came back to a TV blaring wide open and a locked bedroom door. I began to suspect my parents of sexual intercourse.

Think about it. Neither one of them had a reputation for napping. They'd finally come out around suppertime, scramble up some eggs or heat up leftovers. Anything you'd ask, they'd just smile and say yes honey. Sleepovers. *Twilight Zone* reruns. That new litter of kittens born behind the gas station. The little one, Daddy. The calico runt with six toes.

And I wanted to know why. Not what went where. Not ovums and embryos and guppy-looking sperms. Not God's plan, male and female created he them. I wanted the truth of it, the reason people still kept at it the way they did when I knew they no more wanted babies than they did a plague of boils.

I pondered Alleen's monkey-bar revelation on my walk home from school. I made up my mind to ask Connie Lee. She had never lied to me before and I could not say that about many of the adults I knew.

Connie Lee stood watching a *Dialing for Dollars* dinosaur movie from over the counter while she shook a brown paper bag filled with flour, salt, and a cutup fryer. Waiting till the chicken rested on the plate, I phrased my question carefully. "Connie Lee," I asked, looking her in the eye, "what makes people do sex when they don't want babies?"

She stopped halfway between the sink and the stove, her fingertips breaded white and sticky. Hooking a rung of a kitchen chair with her bare foot, she pulled it out and motioned for me to sit. She rinsed her hands at the kitchen sink for a long time, picking the flour out from under each nail. She dried her hands on the dishtowel and sat down in my mother's chair.

"Baby," she sighed, looking from her feet to my face, "when a man and a woman starts kissing way out like that, it's like everything around 'em just starts comin' down all over inside and . . ." She paused. "Honey, you better ax your momma. I might could tell you now, but it'll be better if you wait and ax your momma when she gets home."

But I never did ask. I waited the way you wait when you know someone's following you. Like if I looked back fast enough, I might see the shadow of sex or glimpse its coattail before it disappeared. Every year it snuck up closer, rustling just a little ways off.

I thought maybe it had something to do with the school nurse's "You're a young lady now" presentation. We knew she was going to embarrass us beyond juvenile endurance when she came in wheeling a projector on a rickety metal stand and Mrs. Cole sent the boys out for an afternoon of relay races.

I don't remember much of what the nurse said, even though I listened up good. All I got was something about keeping ourselves clean and how the blood would stop long enough for us to take baths. I do recall looking around the room and seeing my thirteen female classmates, mouths gaping in horror, as our tormentor snapped an elastic sanitary belt on a mannequin and demonstrated how the ends of the pad wound through and around the catches almost like the four-in-hand I'd perfected for my brother's Sunday tie.

Having been a charter member of Alleen's secret club in the second grade, I already knew how the belts and pads worked. She'd brought one of each to school in the second grade and told five of us that to be in her club we had to wear it for a solid hour. I had taken the eleven to noon shift when I wouldn't have to walk around much, then handed it off to Nonnie Myers under a stall in the girls' bathroom, glad to be shed of the contraption.

The following summer, something happened that brought the mystery more into focus for me. Alleen's parents and mine took us swimming out at a lake near Cottondale. Alleen and I ran to the concession stand. We each ordered a suicide, a concoction made by mixing four drinks—Coca-Cola, 7Up, root beer, and something orange. We enjoyed the danger sound of the word, like something a gangster would order.

The young woman behind the counter scowled as she looked up from her Archie comic. Shaking her head, she muttered, "You white people drink anything." Her hair, a complex architecture of cornrows, converged in a knot on top of her head. I figured her for sixteen, working a summer job she hated. She wore a work smock longer than her cut-off blue jean shorts. She filled two Dixie cups with ice, squirted in the syrups, hosed in the soda water, and shoved me my change.

Alleen and I ran to the jukebox. Three songs for a quarter, and my daddy had told us we could play any three we wanted as long as none of them were "Ahab the Arab." I punched in B-9 three times. "Locomotion." Little Eva, a sixteen-year-old black girl from Belhaven, North Carolina, had recorded it while babysitting for Carole King's kids. Carole sang backup.

Alleen and I tried to follow Little Eva's instructions, leaving sandy footprints on the smooth boards of the dance floor. You gotta swing your hips now ooooooo, c'mon baby. Jump up. Jump back. The girl behind the concession stand watched us with disdain, leaning her elbows on the counter and tapping her foot. When the song started again, I guess she just could not stand it anymore.

She reached behind her back, untied the smock, and laid it on the counter, walked over and took us each by the hand.

"Watch me," she ordered. We tried to do what she was doing, starting with the feet and moving up.

By the time we got the hip moves in rhythm with our feet, the song had started for the third time. She let us go and started showing us hand motions. Her tight abdominal muscles flashed between her waistband and the pink shirt she wore knotted up under her breasts. She threw back her head and shoulders, closed her eyes, and started moving into a whole new territory.

By this time I noticed that a small crowd had gathered, maybe fifteen or twenty white people in bathing suits. A few of the mothers did that not-quite-a-whisper-under-your-breath thing where they lean in close to one another, heads cocked, talking out the sides of their mouths, then laughing. Two younger couples started to try the dance themselves, watching the instructor and shaking their heads.

The expressions on the men's faces ranged from smirking amusement to pained leering to pure-dee dumbstruck slack-jawed lust. When Little Eva started singing about the chugga-chugga motion like a railroad train, the girl did an almost undetectable knee bend, starting an undulation at her ankle and rolling it up her dark body. And it traveled smooth and slow. Alleen's mother grabbed her daddy's arm and headed back for the beach so fast his feet got tangled up.

Then the music stopped. The dancer surveyed her audience, gave them a look that went past proud but stopped just short of defiant, and bowed. A few of the men applauded as they dispersed. My father kept watching for a minute or two, taking out a pack of cigarettes, packing them sharply against his palm, and lighting one before he turned away. The dancer walked back behind the counter, slipped her smock back on, and started thumbing through her comic, trying to find her place again.

I knew that I had witnessed sex that day at the lake just as surely as Alleen had seen it on her living room sofa, only in a subtler guise. In a form that would not play as well by the monkey bars. And I wanted it. I did not want to be a dancer in front of crowds of men. I did not want to be black. What I wanted had to do with that expression on her face, that confidence. The knowledge that she could use something she had to tilt the immeasurably uneven balance of power in her own favor.

We went back to Lake Payne three more times that summer. We never mentioned the dance again, but every time I ordered a drink, the dancer pushed my coins back at me. "Suicide's on the house today," she'd say.

In junior high, we studied sex with a diligence we seldom applied to other subjects. Jinkie and May and I passed a worn copy of the lyrics to "Louie Louie" back and forth till the paper felt like a Kleenex. Gets her thrills on top of me? I thought the man got on top. Nah, that's only if you want to get pregnant. You get on top when you're just doing it for fun. By the end of ninth grade, we'd graduated to our brothers' *Playboys,* to *True Confessions,* and the hot parts of John Updike's *Couples.* We took the *Cosmopolitan* quiz every month. How sexy are you? What is your kissing style?

Before too long a couple of us were itching to try it for real. By our junior year of high school, we knew two things for certain: you don't want to get pregnant and the right pills can keep that from happening. Alabama had some of the most liberal abortion laws in the country. A woman could take care of her problem safely and legally if she paid two psychiatrists to say it would be detrimental to her mental health to continue the pregnancy. Still, none of us wanted to do time in those stirrups if we could avoid it. A gynecologist over the river in Northport would prescribe a year's worth of birth control pills to girls under eighteen if they brought a note from their mother.

We begged Angie Darnell to get such a note. Angie looked a lot like Mary Wilson of the Supremes and often bragged to us about how her cool mom would let her do anything—stay out after midnight, wear fishnet stockings to school, and even smoke pot in the den as long as it wasn't a school night. We had to promise her we'd pay her twice the price of the pills and the doctor's visit before she agreed to ask.

She came to school the next day glaring at us, sullen and evil. She avoided Livvie and me in homeroom, but I managed to catch up with her after algebra. "Well?" I asked, dreading the answer. "What happened?"

What had happened was that Angie had been involved in a head-on collision with her mom's coolness limit. "I told her Southwind had broke up with me because I wouldn't do it. Said being a virgin was getting in my way and I wanted some pills.

'In your way?' she started hollering. 'In your WAY? It ain't in your goddamn way. It's way down there between your legs. And it BETTER not be in anyone else's way neither!' Then she grabbed my sister's doll off the floor and started waling the shit outta me with Malibu Barbie. See here?" She pulled down the back collar of her shirt and showed us a crop of five or six double bruises on her shoulder. I gathered that Mrs. Darnell had held Barbie by the head.

"Oh, god, Angie. I'm so sorry!" Livvie said, reaching out to touch the bruises.

Angie jerked away, her eyes narrowed. "You white bitches go get your own damn pills and leave me out of it."

And in the end, that's what we white bitches did. To get us started, May stole a handful of sample packs from her GP's office while she waited in the exam room for her yearly physical. Livvie made the big score, though, when she appealed to her stepmother, who decided to save time and give notes to her and both of her sisters. Neither of them had any concerns about spawning yet, so Livvie, May, Jinkie, and I divvied them up, paying with our babysitting money.

Each of us kept our green plastic sample cases with the cameo profiles in our locker. We learned from Jinkie's older cousin that you could toss the last seven tablets in the pack and take the others every day and you'd skip your period. May, Jinkie, and I only did this once in a while. May skipped hers for a swim meet and Jinkie for a weekend trip to see the Allman Brothers in New Orleans, but Livvie, always one to take things to extremes, didn't have a period her whole senior year.

Norinyl 1+80. Drug companies made stronger pills back then. By the time we needed them for contraception, I bet we had enough residual hormones floating around our bodies to render a she-bison sterile. Probably a good thing, since we were less than diligent about taking them regularly. We skipped them, swapped them, then doubled or tripled them up and gulped them down like M&Ms.

All four of us had grown up with a deep and abiding faith in the benevolence of drugs. Enough time had lapsed for the thalidomide babies in *Life* magazine to slip our minds completely. We had all lined up in the school cafeteria as children to suck on Dr. Sabin's sugar cubes so we wouldn't get polio. We trusted drugs so much that when Bobbi Jenkins read us that warning about tetracycline increasing your photosensitivity, we started hoarding those, too. We'd pop a few yellow and blue capsules each before going to the pool so we would tan faster. The right pill could render us ready for just about anything.

And to make certain of our readiness, we practiced. On each other. Not a lot and never past a certain point. Often it happened when one of us had broken up with some boy we'd been dating. We'd hold each other for comfort in our rooms with the doors shut, ask for advice. Sometimes cry a little. Whisper what he'd begged me to do. Maybe he broke up with me because I'm not a good kisser. Here. Show me. Try this next time. Just think of it as practicing for the real thing.

Practice sessions got so popular in some circles that Sallie Fitts's mother regretted the peek she took into the rec room to see why the girls at Sallie's slumber party had gotten so quiet. Rumor had it she staggered into a tableau vivant that resembled a whorehouse on nickel night, and not one y chromosome in the ménage. Several of the guests did not show their faces at school Monday morning. And poor Mrs. Fitts. She'd been going to twelve-step meetings for months to try and wean herself off Valium and the incident bumped her all the way back to admitting she was powerless.

By our senior year, my friend May and I shifted gears from considering intercourse to ready to cha-cha. Our approach was cold-blooded. "It's just something you have to learn to do to get on with your life," May told me, "like parallel parking or frying chicken." I just didn't want to get pregnant, get burned, or run into anything too expensive. And none of us wanted to look stupid doing it.

We also had to overcome the obstacle of finding an appropriate partner, someone competent and tolerable. None of us could imagine doing it with any of the high school boys we had dated, and most of the college boys ran with their hair in flames when they saw us coming, with good reason. We had reached the point of considering crossing the Black Warrior River to check out the farmboy prospects at County High when my eyes lit on Tom.

Livvie knew him from children's theater. They had performed together in *Midsummer Night's Dream*. Nice guy, she said. Played bass in a jazz band. He did not pick on black students nor did he avoid them. Smart, quiet, and sort of a loner, all of which made him stand out in the pep rally culture of Tuscaloosa High.

People in town said his mother used to be a beatnik up in Greenwich Village. When Tom missed a day of school and had to bring a note explaining his absence, she wrote him the best excuse in the history of Tuscaloosa High. I saw it myself, as I escaped homeroom by working in the office in the morning. "Please excuse Tom's absence from school. He did not come to school because he hates your school."

Some said he had been in trouble before, involved with a biology student teacher. He was also rumored to have been involved with drugs, with a mulatto waitress, even with an older man. Tom was rumored to have been involved, period. He walked with grace and confidence, and his smile came so easy.

Livvie and I walked to the door of the smoking porch and stood at the screen. No girls allowed. Tom leaned against a column in his scuffed brown leather coat, watching a herd of sophomore boys engaged in sweaty combat to see who could spit a partially chewed brownie against the wall with enough force to make it stick. Hanging brownies, they called it. Tom stood at a distance from them, his expression hovering between amazement and disgust.

He stood up straight and smiled, came right over when Livvie called out to him. "Tom, this is Melissa. I've been meaning to introduce the two of you."

Tom took my hand, squeezed it slightly. "Pleasure," he said, then reached in his pocket and took out a pack of Winstons. My father's brand. Never breaking eye contact, he began tapping the pack against his palm to tamp the tobacco down. And there she was, taking her bow. That long-ago dancer from Lake Payne locomoted through my mind. I can do this, I thought. I lifted my chin a little.

"Nice jacket," I said, lowering my voice to pass for cool.

Often over the next two weeks, Tom drove me in a green MG convertible he borrowed from his mother's boyfriend, a guy named Dieter who taught English lit at the university. Tom laughed. He spoke with an absence of self-consciousness I had never seen in a boy my own age. Dieter would lend him just about anything, Tom said—the car, money, his apartment—to get Tom out of the house.

Sometimes instead of going straight home, we drove out into the country after school to Lake Nichol or to Deerlick Creek. We walked forest trails and smoked pot. Once we paddled a friend's rowboat around Forest Lake. I liked the way he held out his hand to help me into the wobbling boat, naturally, casually, as if he did not have to think about doing it. He rowed hard straight toward the side of a dock, then laid down the oars and pulled me down flat onto the bottom of the boat, and we drifted under with maybe a foot of clearance, staring up at sky, then at dark sludge and the wet, barnacled wood. Side by side we inhaled the cool fungal smell, then squinted when the sunshine assailed us again as we glided out on the other side.

We had fun the way children do after school, going outside to play. Of course we attended the requisite dances, the occasional party, and even a football game or two, but our dates were never the hamburger, movie, and make-out tussles other boys favored. By the time Tom and I started kissing one afternoon in a way that meant let's go ahead, I trusted him. We drove south over the Hale county line to Moundville.

At its peak in the middle of the thirteenth century, one of the largest American cities north of Mexico prospered in central west Alabama on the banks of the Black Warrior River. Of course, nobody called it Moundville then. Nobody knows what the inhabitants did call it. They lived among some two dozen flat-topped earthen mounds laid out in a soft rectangle. Some archaeologists believe that the site evolved into a way station for the journey from one world to the next, a necropolis where people brought their dead to priests who specialized in conveying them safely into the afterlife. Whatever went on there, the reason for the city's abandonment remains a mystery as well. By 1500, deer and mosquitoes had claimed the site as their own.

Over 450 years later, every schoolchild in Alabama had eaten at least one baloney sandwich on top of the biggest mound. The field trip to Moundville glows forever in the minds of those of us who peered down over that cool concrete wall into the museum's open burial pit display. Eight years old, I started counting skulls to see how many of the ancient dead rested there, and made it to fourteen before Ronnie Dunn dropped a Golden Flake potato chip bag over the edge and got us all flung out. They closed up that display in 1989 and I don't damn blame them.

Tom parked Dieter's MG near the chain-locked gate that blocked the road after hours. We walked through the pines. I had never entered the park without a busload of kids or a Buick full of squabbling relatives. Not a long walk in, but a hot one, and by the time we got to the covered pavilion, I could see peach in the sky. We rested on a splintery bench, holding hands, wordless and sweat-shiny, watching dirt daubers dance around their nests in the rafters until we caught our breath for the climb. The fountain did not work, but Tom found a spigot around back of the museum and disconnected the hosepipe, and we bent down one at a time to drink lukewarm sulphur-scented water.

We could not see the Black Warrior through the trees as we climbed, but we could smell it and hear the way wind and animal sounds echoed off the water. Two steep trails of hard-packed red dirt led up the tallest mound. We took the far one. Sixty feet up at a sharp incline, topped by two level acres of foot-tall weeds.

Maybe we would have felt shy in a cooler season, but in that heat we both started unbuttoning without ceremony. Tom spread his shirt over the top of the pile of jeans and I laid mine over his. We both lay down, mostly on fabric, and did what we climbed up to do. This is it, this is it, I kept thinking, and suddenly I recalled the day I found a shed snakeskin nine years earlier close to where we lay.

Twenty-five shrieking children had chased one another on top of the mound, whooping and wielding their souvenir tomahawks while our teacher and two volunteer mothers kept us away from the perimeter. Looking over Tom's shoulder, I could almost see them, herding us like border collies, away from the edge. I'd held the snakeskin high while Deborah Kay Bonner took a picture of me with her Kodak Instamatic, me showing off and laughing until Mrs. Hobson hollered, "Melissa Joyce Delbridge, you drop that filthy thing." She made me write sentences when we got back on the bus. I will not pick up nasty dead animals. Forty-seven times, and it would have been a hundred if I hadn't gotten carsick. And by the time I finished all that remembering, everything had gotten still except for the crickets. You wouldn't think fireflies would venture up that high, but some did.

What Tom and I did did not hurt, nor did it feel particularly good. Both of these facts surprised me, but I figured I'd get used to it. I did like making Tom happy, and he seemed to enjoy it so much. What I liked best was him smoothing his shirt down, like his hand could soften the denim and buttons into something special for me. That, and his arm around me on the hike back to the car and all the way home.

I know I should have been in love with Tom, but I wasn't. I just did not want to wait any longer. I chose as best I could given the prospects at hand, and I could have done much worse. That night, I steeped in the bathtub for nearly an hour. And I went through a whole bottle of clear nail polish over the coming week, painting dots over chigger bites in places impolite to scratch.

So I plunged first. Jinkie ran a close second with Neal, a County High football player she'd mooned over for a year, much as a girl like Jinkie could moon. She did it with him three Friday nights in a row before he dumped her for some titless wonder blonde who went to his church.

Jinkie consoled herself by impersonating his mother with Oscar-worthy accuracy, calling the phone company, and having his phone number changed to an unlisted one on a Friday afternoon. Three days passed before they figured out why nobody could call in and convinced Southern Bell to tell them their own phone number. Not long after that, Jinkie ran off to Atlanta and she never did come back for good.

Livvie, set on beefing up her theatrical resume, auditioned and memorized lines more than she flirted, but May would have jumped off the deep end sooner than I if she had managed to light a fire under Sean. Her age made him cautious, I guess. She met him at a quad concert his sophomore year at the university. His attraction to May surprised none of us. She had short curly hair the color of rose gold, bright foxlike eyes, and a figure that managed to achieve both curves and athleticism. The kind of looks that made cautious men wish she were fair game. Still, no matter how hard she tried to seduce him, he would not comply.

After Jinkie left, May and I grew closer. Our humanities teacher, a young red-head who wore macramé belts, inspired us with a genuine enthusiasm about the arts. When I didn't go creekbanking with Tom, May and I passed the afternoons together, swooning over Ann Sexton's *Love Poems,* T. S. Eliot's, or perfecting charcoal renderings of Bernini's *Ecstasy of St. Theresa.* In between, we practiced rolling the perfect joint, eschewing E-Z Widers for the classic simplicity of Tops or the elegance of 1.25 JOB Silver Lights.

May liked Tom, approved of our relationship. I filled her in on the details on nights when I slept at her house. I loved her room. Once the sleeping porch of their Victorian house, it ran the length of the second floor. Three windowed walls flooded the room with leaf-filtered light in the morning, and a vintage wrought-iron space heater warmed it on winter nights, its back grid glowing like the windows of a miniature cathedral. We slept in a high iron bed covered by a crazy quilt her great-grandmother had stitched from random shapes of embroidered velvet.

We laid in supplies on Friday afternoon—Goo-Goo Clusters, cans of cashews, Winstons, sweet fizzy Matteus wine we paid the shoe-shine man to buy for us. After midnight, we twisted colored candles into the mouths of the fat empty bottles. We lined them up on her dresser, lighting joints from them, dreaming and watching the wax flow down, playing "Suite Judy Blue Eyes" till we knew the skips as well as we knew the lyrics.

Of course I confided in May about what Tom and I were doing. Best friends did back then. We were lounging around on her bed late at night. "Maybe it gets more fun when you get better at it. I don't know. I mean, it's not . . . it's just . . ." I floundered for the right way to say it, then gave up.

May took a deep draw on her Winston, exhaled, and looked up at the ceiling. "You ever thought about what it would be like to try it with a girl?"

Her question jolted me so hard that I flicked my ash on her great-grandmother's quilt and had to bend down to blow it off so it would not leave a smear.

"Oh, sure," I answered, trying to hide how her question unnerved me. "Vicki told me all about what went on at Sallie's slumber party. Said she had a great time."

"What did you think about it?"

I smiled and shrugged. "Just wished I'd been nicer to Sallie and maybe she'd have invited me."

May laughed and shifted her pillows under her neck. "Well, I knew two girls who . . ."

We talked this way for maybe an hour, talked around the edges of what she was suggesting, until I finally summoned as much courage as I'd ever had to whistle up. "May?" I asked. "You want to give it a go?"

May took a hit off her cigarette, a long deep hit, like she had to consider her answer carefully.

For a moment I panicked, envisioning her telling the whole school, imagining my life as a nasty rumor. Tom might leave me. Maybe even Livvie would not want me for a friend.

Then May exhaled, and as she did, her fingers started in on the top button of her pajama top. Then the top button of mine.

"I tell you what," she whispered, "You just lie back and I won't do anything really heavy."

But she did. And I finally understood what Connie Lee had told me in the kitchen so long ago. We started kissing way out like that, and I never even had to think about what to do next, because everything around me just started coming down all over. That girl turned me inside out and I simmered with it for nearly a year.

Knowing now how it was supposed to work, I thought it would get better with Tom. He and I still did it once a week or so, usually at Dieter's apartment. Of course, May had known all about Tom and me. After a few weeks, as he and I walked the fern path at the arboretum, I confessed to Tom about her.

"Wow," Tom said, nodding his head with the nonchalance of the hip. "That sounds really beautiful, the two of you . . ." He trailed off, stoned and smiling. No jealousy, no shock, and, to his credit, no request for a ringside seat. The only wrinkle in the fabric of my life during this time was the necessity of avoiding my stepfather's advances and bullying. My two lovers fortified me, providing a refuge he could not violate.

Soon Sean and May and Tom and I began double dating. Until the spring, we went out together every Friday night. At the end of the evening, the guys kissed us goodnight at May's front door. She and I tiptoed, drunk and giggling, up the creaking stairs and into her room where we fell into one another's arms.

Then up slithered the serpent. Every garden has one. May came into school on Monday morning, shiny-eyed and chirping. "Sean and I. Last night."

I raised my eyebrows.

She nodded. I watched her mouth as she spoke. I tried to achieve an expression of enthusiasm and excitement for her. "I'm so happy for the two of you," I lied, not wanting to appear unsophisticated. And I realized for the first time that I often felt as if I had to pretend to be more detached than I was with May. I listened to her talk about Sean every time I saw her that day. I smiled and asked what I hoped were the right questions. After each conversation, I plotted flaying Sean alive, sneaking into his student hovel and throttling him in his sleep.

I started spending less time with May. We still made love once in a while. She would call to ask if Tom and I wanted to go with them to a movie or to hear a band. "Should I bring an overnight bag?" I'd ask, trying to sound casual. I hated having to ask and hated waiting for her answer. Sometimes she said, "Of course!" as if nothing had changed between us. Other times she hesitated, and I imagined her finger pointing back and forth. Eeny-meeny-miney-mo. If she answered, "Oh, don't bother. Sean and I will probably hang out later," I'd pretend indifference to the snub, ask what she was wearing to the movie.

But I kept score in my heart. Did she want more nights with him or with me? More and more I could not stand the image of her whispering into his ear, of Sean holding her, of him tracing the almost invisible down on the skin of her lower back. And I hated the hypocrite I had turned out to be, unable to return her acceptance of my relationship with Tom.

I ended it three weeks later on a morning in March. We were sitting on a bench in the park by the school. "You have to choose. Him or me," I told her in tears, despising the clichéd words flopping like toads out of my mouth. I knew she'd choose him before I finished the demand and hoped I was wrong. I was not.

"Oh, Melissa. Don't make me do this." She smiled sadly at me, shaking her head and shrugging her pink sweater closer around her shoulders. She held onto my arm when I turned away.

"Sean," she said, "can offer me things you can't."

"No shit!" I muttered.

"I don't mean that." She spoke softly, without cruelty. "He has his own place, a job. I mean, look at us. We're kids. We don't even have cars . . ."

Then I was too far away to hear the rest of what she said.

I never once spoke to May after that. A few days later, I received the first of three notes from her, asking me to reconsider. I found them stuffed through the grate of my locker, covered with a messy blush of her kisses. In the saddest, she wrote, "I can't stand school without you being mine. I miss your funny notes, your smile every morning. I'll abide by your wishes, but my heart won't be in it and my life won't ever be the same."

Whose would? I never answered and her notes stopped. About a week later, May did not show up at school. She'd left with Sean a month before graduation, taken off for either Greenville, South Carolina, or Quebec, depending on who was telling the story. I almost went batshit crazy with rage and the loss of her before finally grabbing my own bootstraps. A month of grief, then I woke up one morning bored with misery. I could not stand hurting like that any more. Catch hold and toughen up, big girl, I chided myself in the mirror. You read the poem. In the room, the women come and go.

I kept dating Tom a while longer, still not in love, but needing his friendship and familiarity. When I found his note in my locker, thanking me and explaining that he was moving to San Francisco with Dieter, loss flooded over me again, but this time it washed off clean and fast, and a tingle of freedom came soaring right behind.

I rode my bike to the quad after school and sat on the steps of Denny Chimes to smoke what Tom had left me folded into his note. There, I thought. That's done. And I'm a world-class parallel parker. If I could just learn to fry chicken I'd have everything aced.

"Now what I'm about to tell you is the gospel truth," Momma Reba slurred her words only slightly. My stepmother insisted that I call her that. A year had passed since graduation, and Livvie and I had stopped by her place for brunch. Daddy had taken off on one of his dubious hunting trips. He'd run halfway through his fourth marriage by then and Reba'd slid halfway through her third Bloody Mary of the morning. A good-looking black-haired woman in her midforties, she'd inherited enough money from her father's pawn shops and natural gas wells to finance her periodic stays in some of the finer substance-abuse facilities in the southeastern United States.

She reached up to pull down on her bra where the underwire was cutting into her ribcage, elbowing a potted red geranium off the gazebo railing and onto the lawn. She gazed down after it, shaking her head as if it had jumped, then continued her gossip about the wife of a local politician. "You remember Burt Darden's wife Ellie? Used to water-ski down at Cypress Gardens?" We nodded. "Well, honey, he came home early from a fund-raising trip and walked right in on her going at it with her tennis instructor. A woman!"

"What did he do?" I asked. This brunch was turning out to be a lot more fun than I'd anticipated, in spite of the slightly burnt quiche crust.

"Well, I reckon he didn't know what to do," she replied. "He like to fell out. He walked out and fixed himself a cocktail and waited till he heard the back door slam and a car start, then went back and sat down on the bed. He's a fool about Ellie. Always has been.

"He told her nice as he could, honey, I understand how this could happen, me on the road so much and all. She just there stood in front of the mirror, trying to make her hair presentable. Maybe we need more time together, he told her. A vacation might do us some good. She kept on patting and spraying, patting and spraying and he just kept on forgiving.

"And bless Pat if she didn't fling her hairbrush at him and holler fuck you and your vacation, Burt. And before he had time to wind his watch she vacated her hot little ass right on down to Boca Raton with that tennis hussy."

"Well," Livvie deadpanned, "poor old Ellie. I guess she probably needed lots of help with her game. I played doubles with her once and she never could serve for shit."

Her joke whizzed right on past Momma Reba. So much did. She shook her head with bitterness. "No, darling. It was not tennis. You girls are still young, but you would not believe it. There's so much of that shit going on in Tuscaloosa you're bound to step in it sooner or later. You can't even go in the ladies' dressing room at the country club anymore, it's gotten so bad around here."

Livvie and I avoided each other's eyes. She slipped off her flip-flop under the table and tickled my ankle with her toes. Reba, Reba, I laughed in my mind, glowing with all the sin and wisdom and conde-scension of nineteen years. Honey, it's been that bad around here my whole damn life. You just ain't been stepping in the right places.

Girls Turned In

Sensing menace, a snail or a turtle will suck back into its own shell faster than you'd think it could move. Blink and you'll miss it. Girls mistreated do something similar, only slower. They turn in on themselves when things get too bad, and it breaks your heart to see it happen. I worked in the mental health field for years after college. I learned different names for it depending on how it manifests. What a girl does is scrunch back down inside herself so tightly that nobody in the world can get a hold on her anymore. A boy, he's more likely to pick up his hunting rifle and make meat of his girlfriend's parents or teach his mean classmates a last tough lesson in the school cafeteria, but a girl—usually she'll just turn in on herself.

Nobody much likes to point out this sort of thing till it gets bad. If it sneaks up on her, you can't tell exactly when it happens. Maybe she's always been a little unusual. You don't want to go so far as to say odd, or pry too much. Before you know it, her hair's wild, full of knots, and her head is tilting funny. Maybe she quits looking you in the eye. Picking up pinecones becomes her passion in life. Something simple and harmless, something nobody can fault her for doing.

Or maybe the sun goes down and comes back up again and there she sits on the front porch, wetting her pants and the glider cushion, just floating back and forth like nothing's changed. Eventually somebody—a social worker from the state or a family friend or the husband of the lady her momma used to work for—comes and carries her off to Bryce's so she won't embarrass anybody. Whatever went wrong for her, she will probably keep quiet about it. People might talk, but just to each other and not to anyone involved. No witnesses to what caused it all and it will just stay hidden till before you know it she's flat turned in on herself.

Towns have institutions that define them. Tuscaloosa had three, all built along the banks of the Black Warrior River. Jack Warner's Gulf States Paper Company stunk up the whole town and employed many of its citizens; the University of Alabama—white-haired professors and the Crimson Tide—gave us a reason to hold up our heads; and Bryce Hospital haunted us, hovered over us somewhere between a nightmare, a joke in poor taste, and the worst threat you could imagine.

Every last one of us knew it did not take a lot to end up there, and we knew people—both your forensic types and your inconvenient family members—who had. People who got sent to Bryce's might be mentally retarded (and thus really belonging more at Partlow a mile or so further down the Birmingham Highway), brain damaged, or mentally ill. "Not quite right," in the parlance of the time. My people lived in Pine Park Circle, right across the highway and a few blocks down. Native Tuscaloosans called it Bryce's, not Bryce Hospital, and that's how you could tell locals from people who came to quarterback for Bear or study or teach at the university. One of the ways.

People around town had observed the close relationship between Bryce's and the university since the early days of each. State officials first named it the Alabama Hospital for the Insane (Alabama being a spade-is-a-spade sort of state). In the *Meteor,* July 4, 1872, a publication edited by Bryce patients, an anonymous inmate wrote the following in an article entitled "Magnetism":

> The University and Hospital for the Insane may be regarded as representing the two Poles of the great intellectual Magnet of the State. The grounds of the two institutions join, and their buildings loom over the landscape as if rising to take a side view of each other. Let us glance at some differences that distinguish them.
>
> The inmates of the University come to acquire ideas. We come to get rid of them. They receive encomiums for proficiency in military tactics. The slightest proclivities in that direction, at our house, insure rebuke. If a student is insubordinate or irregular in his deportment, he is sent home. The more obstreperous our behavior, the closer we are held.

Mrs. Garland, the wife of the president of the university, stood in the high dome of the brand-new hospital with her friends Dr. Peter

Bryce and his wife to watch Croxton's Raiders hit town with a vengeance in April of 1865. People say she ran home from her perch when she saw smoke rising from campus and stopped the Union troops from torching the president's mansion. If there is truth to this, the woman made record time. It took me fifteen minutes to ride my bike from that side of campus to the pistachio tree on the lawn at Bryce's, and I was on wheels and pavement, not running across a muddy Alabama field in April, encumbered by umpteen pounds of skirt and a corset to boot. Then again, I suppose I lacked Mrs. Bryce's motivation. When the Yankees reached the hospital grounds, Dr. Bryce met them at the gate. They confiscated the livestock, causing great hardship, but did no further harm to the buildings, patients, or staff.

The first patient, with his diagnosis of "political excitability," arrived in 1861. Both the structure itself and the treatments offered there were state-of-the-art. Before the completion of the Pentagon in 1943, Bryce's covered more land area than any other building in the United States. Only administrative offices are housed in the old building now, patients living in more modern secure facilities.

Dr. Thomas Story Kirkbride designed the structure. Like eagles' wings, wards zigzagged out from either side of three porticoed stories capped with a grand dome. Every ward had long wide halls, airy porches, fresh-air ducts, and twenty-two-foot ceilings. Peter Bryce, a twenty-six-year-old gentleman doctor from South Carolina, brought his young bride, the former Ellen Clarkson, to Tuscaloosa when he became the hospital's first director. A proponent of humane care of inmates, he emphasized the importance of treating patients with courtesy, kindness, and respect, using no unnecessary shackles or restraints. Work programs of sewing and farming provided therapeutic and meaningful activities and helped make ends meet during the war.

Dr. Bryce believed that the grounds should be like a park, soothing to the troubled mind and spirit. His sweet wife took great interest in the planting of fruit trees, nut trees, and shade trees. Of the ornamental trees, the Chinese pistache was her pride and joy.

Go to Tuscaloosa in the autumn and ask about the pistachio tree, and anyone will give you directions right to it, even though it is not really a pistachio. For one thing, it's huge. The trunk measures 133 inches in circumference today and stands over 54 feet tall with a branch span of 71 feet. In spite of its height you can only see it from inside the fence because of the long drive from the gate to the main building. I learned as a schoolgirl how to look up our tree on the National Register of Historic Trees. I imagined Mrs. Bryce supervising its planting in the springtime, dressed like Scarlett O'Hara, showing a trusted inmate or a servant (she would have been too well-mannered to call a slave a slave) where to dig, how to water and mulch the sapling. The leaves changing from green to their shocking golden orange must have brought her tremendous pleasure during those first years.

Over a century later, my mother drove me on autumn Sunday afternoons to admire the tree. She'd pull over and stop outside the gate. "Lock your door, precious, and close your eyes." I'd feel the car roll forward at a nearly imperceptible speed. And when she told me to open, I would see the tree before I'd see the harmless patients, the ones with grounds passes shuffling past us with their overmedicated palsies and their snuff-blackened teeth.

Drive by and have a look. They'll let you right in, and it's something to see. The color of the leaves simply stuns, almost too brilliant to bear. Like a cloud fell out of the sky, caught fire on the way down, and hovered there burning just before touching the earth.

Walking down to the corner store to buy our Pixy Stix and Yoo-Hoos, we would run into town-card patients ("residents," we called them after 1971, when the federal government came in and taught us better) on their way to buy their Beech-Nut or their Skoal. We kids never counted crazy a bad word, although we knew lots of clever euphemisms. My mother used "a cup and saucer short of having a full place setting." When we saw patients coming, we'd help them cross the street, then make a motion as if sipping tea once they passed, if no grownups stood in swatting range. Sometimes they looked or acted strange or tried to hug our necks.

That's the way we were with the town-card holders. We played with them and sometimes they played us. We could watch them and feel superior, or help them and feel merciful. Once in a while, though, those not supposed to get out did. That got to us, kept us up nights or at least made us get up to make sure we'd hooked the screen.

Syrup Sopper, the deejay who ran the Swap Shop on the Tuscaloosa AM station, warned us over my grandma's radio when a man prone to violence escaped. We'd be sitting around her kitchen table finishing off last night's leftovers when he'd interrupt his jokes to let us know the man who'd stabbed that nurse with a doubled-up coat hanger had busted out. Once in a while he'd inform listeners in polite terms (not too graphic for little ears) exactly what he'd done to that poor girl in Demopolis. Aunt Mike would get up and call the collie to the front porch.

We children would try to sneak into eavesdropping range to get the details the grownups whispered about so we could act out the parts in the playhouse my daddy had built us. "Okay, Beverly. I'll be the poor girl in Demopolis and you be the one that found her. Take this coat hanger, Johnnie Lee, and you be the crazy man from Bryce's. Here. Here's where I answer the door. Play like this shoebox is the cinder block you try to bust over my head." In cases like that, everybody'd sleep better once we heard he got caught stealing potted meat at the Jitney Jungle.

Ending up at Bryce's could be your own fault or it might be your family's or it might be something nobody could help. However it happened, you came to Tuscaloosa if you lived in Alabama and something just wasn't quite right about you or if something went bad wrong along the way.

A couple of members of my family knew the place from the inside. A few times a year, we would go to visit Aunt Luella (really my second cousin) there. Momma let me gather pecans outside long as I stayed where she could see me from the window. Aunt Luella, she explained, was not crazy. She got put there because if you didn't watch her she'd drink more than a lady should. Also because she would not sell some land her mother'd left her to the Alabama Highway Department the way Uncle Benny and the rest of the family thought she should. Not right, Momma told me, but that's just the way it was. My sister and I wandered around outside, throwing nuts at one another, not the least bit scared.

Once she decided to sell thirty acres and lay off the liquor, Aunt Luella got out and went back home to live with Aunt Audrey (really my great-aunt). Good days, she might come over and help my mother plant snapdragons and maidenhair ferns in the rock-lined beds at our new ranch house. Bad days, we'd cross town to take them a bone-in ham baked with pineapples, and she wouldn't even come downstairs. Just stayed in her bedroom chain-smoking and hollering down about us bringing charity to our poor relations.

Some said poor little Reba Fain should have gone to Bryce's, that she might still walk among us if she had. Hers was the worst sort of turning in. Such a timid little lank-haired girl, in the same Sunday school class as my sister, eleven when I turned thirteen. Wouldn't ever look you in the eye and too shy to say boo to a goose. Hung herself from the low limb of a sweet gum tree in one of the worst thunderstorms of the spring. Her mother wept into a soaked-through Kleenex at the funeral reception and blamed it on the way Reba's face broke out. "It just worried her so bad," she sobbed. I remember Mr. Fain, the way he'd stand glitter-eyed and licking his lips when girls got on the bus during our church choir tour. Never did believe a skin condition killed Reba. Bryce's might have saved her, I don't know.

My grandmother went to work there as a nurse's aide to help out her family when she was sixteen years old. That was in 1920. She lived in a dormitory with other girls, got half a day off every week, and received gentlemen only with a chaperone. She knew all about Bryce's, and always hoped my Aunt Grace wouldn't end up there. Grace was my father's big sister, grandma's oldest child. They knew from the time she could walk that something was unusual about her, and a doctor told my grandmother that a new surgical procedure might help, but there were risks. My grandfather would not allow it.

Grace had a happy life far as we could tell. As an adult, she stood six foot two and could carry a heavier load than my daddy. She could read enough to enjoy the funny papers and always had a cat or two she smiled at through the kitchen window during the morning and held in her lap at night. I remember her putting up peach preserves and taking jars to the neighbors, who would thank her and make sure she got back across the street all right. Grace could lift us up to reach the high fruit on the trees and never got tired of playing with us. We, in turn, watched over her.

All of us children had to stay away, though, when she had one of her spells. They came on her about once a month, and, as my grandmother explained, they made Grace very nervous. One of her spells snuck up on her one day as we sat around Grandma's dinner table. My sister Shell sat in the high chair kicking the footrest the way a toddler will, and Grace quietly pulled the carving knife out of the smoked ham and starting plodding toward her. My Aunt Mike, who never raised her voice, grabbed Grace with both arms like she was hugging her from behind, and started screaming for me to take Shell home right now. I never told my mother about it, because I knew she wouldn't let us go back over there for a long time. I also knew Grace would be drawing cowboys on torn-open brown paper grocery bags with us again next week. We knew that she loved us and that her spells were a mystery she could not help.

My grandma wore a deep maroon dress to Grace's funeral. At ninety-six, she never wore black because she thought it made her look so old. When I kissed her cheek and told her how beautiful she looked, she laughed at me. "Sugarplum, don't lie to your grandma. I'm ninety-six and this dress is old enough to vote."

We could laugh, all recognizing the miracle, the blessing around us. Grace had died so fast, easy and early, after a quick bout of some sort of diabetic complications. If she had outlasted my grandma or Aunt Mike, with whom she lived all her life, she would have ended up in Bryce's. Psychiatrists and treatment plans would have upset Grace, confused her. She had us instead; people who knew how special she was, and all those peaches to reach and put by, and we loved her so. Grandma hobbled up to the coffin the night they held the visitation, smiled down over her walker at her firstborn. "Bye-bye, sweetheart," she whispered, tenderly like she was tucking her into a cradle.

By the time I worked at Bryce's, things had gone bad, then got better again. In 1971, the investigation started by the Wyatt-Stickney litigation found over two thousand patients (and only three psychiatrists) crammed into a facility that now houses 450. Prodded by one of those federal government mandates, mental health officials in Alabama cleaned things up. They hired some folks, released others, and installed dropped ceilings, as the exposed overhead pipes proved a bad choice for a facility where residents were likely to be on the depressed side. Modern outbuildings replaced most of the wards in the wings.

During a brief stint in graduate school in the special education program in 1977, I took a part-time job in Bryce's Patient Activities Department. My grandmother warned me after breakfast the day I started at Bryce's, "You be careful don't none of them colored boys knock you in the head." And she was as right about the head-knocking as she was wrong to lay it on one race. The boys were often violent. A few of the girls were, too, (and the ones who were would sooner kick your ass than look at you), but lots of them were there for something they could not help, something embarrassing or sexual, or because they simply weren't quite right—turned in on themselves—and because nobody knew what the hell else to do for them.

A few times in my life, I got a chance to help get a girl turned rightside out again. I tried my best, but far as I know they all ended up staying at Bryce's. May be for the best. Back in Tuscaloosa, we weren't afraid of crazy because, like most people, we were more afraid of what we had not seen than we were of what walked around in front of us every day. I never feared crazy, but over the years, I managed to develop a real healthy respect for it.

Some girls turn in young. You'd be surprised. A little girl whose daddy drove her mad sat next to me in the second grade. I'm not sure exactly how he did it, but I'll go to my grave believing it. Every day I tried to help her with her work.

She looked like a tow-headed cupid from a Victorian valentine, all wispy curls and puffed ivory skin with the pink showing through from deep underneath. Her name was Rose, and never once did she speak to me. She wore old-fashioned clothes, perfectly ironed and a little big for her. Immaculate though, like somebody cared. Found-in-the-attic-looking things. Somehow they suited her, and she was beautiful in them.

December being my birthday, the board of education would not let me start school till I was nearly seven. This worked in my favor, although at the time my mother cussed officials to anyone who would listen. Bigger and more mature than most of the kids and eager to learn, I soaked up lessons like no more were coming. I'd get done with my work fast, and once I started reading, Mrs. Harden encouraged me to stop by the round book-table and pick a book when I turned my paper in. Kept me from disturbing the kids around me.

One day I set up *Horton Hatches the Egg* like a screen so my teacher could not see me and started playing with the mercury from a broken thermometer, rolling it around on my fingers. When I saw Rose watching, I put the mercury drop on her desk. She stretched out a babyish finger and began playing, too. Oddly enough, I noticed that she was using exactly the same motion, the same finger I had used. She mimicked me. That's how I figured out how to get her to do some schoolwork.

She'd write or draw whatever I did. If I gave her a piece of paper just like mine and a pencil the same color, she'd copy. At first I'd make a few wrong marks to make it believable, then erase the errors on my paper and hand in the corrected one. After a few days, I told Mrs. Harden about it because I felt like a cheater. She thanked me for being honest with her and especially for being kind to Rose. It was good for Rose, she thought, to participate instead of just look at her desktop all day.

So I just kept on writing big and clear and pushing my paper over where she could see it. I kept the book screen up, not to hide, but because Rose would only copy when the book was up and nobody was watching. "That's real good, Rose," I'd tell her, and I gave her my stewed apricots whenever we had them with our thirty-five-cent school lunch. I did not like cooked fruit anyway. Once in a while I'd give her a sugar cookie if I had two, and she solemnly ate it, fat sugar crystals and yellow crumbs sticking to her lips and chin. Just stayed there all day waiting to be wiped away.

Helping Rose made me so proud, like I'd figured out how to open a safe everyone thought was locked up for good. Soon, I noticed the way she'd stand outside the school facing the front door until I arrived, even on cold mornings. Got to where she'd never go in without me.

Today they'd diagnose Rose as autistic. Hell, close to catatonic. She would go wherever you led her without resistance, sit there like a knot on a log no matter what you said or did.

The house Rose's family rented backed onto the school playground so we could see their junky backyard from our classroom window. They kept a poor old rib-racked cur chained up to a ramshackle shed. Every time you'd look out the window he'd be trying to scratch a place he couldn't reach or gnawing on something.

Rose's daddy reminded me of the trolls in our fairy-tale books, like something that might live under a bridge and threaten little girls who tried to cross. Short and bearded with a big belly that lapped way over his belt. He looked older than most of my friends' dads, and long white hairs stuck out of his chin and cheeks.

Every day during recess, Rose's daddy stumbled out the back door, stepped down a cinder-block stoop into the mud, tripped over a rusted-out radiator or a busted shovel, and stood in front of the schoolyard's chain-link fence until we came running. Reaching into his pocket, he'd pull out a long blue balloon and begin to blow. Always blue balloons. We watched him make animals from them.

Silent as his daughter, he handed them over the fence to the girls in the prettiest dresses. They clamored to get to the front. Lynn Brandon and Cherry Jennings, resplendent in their frills and petticoats, got them all the time—baby elephants and monkeys eating blue bananas. Once in a while a boy who asserted himself might score a dachshund. I bet I saw him make three or four animals every day between September and early February that year, and never once did he give one to his own little girl, or wink at her or call her sugarplum. Rose hung back at the edge of the crowd, facing the same direction as the other children but not really watching him at all.

I only got a balloon animal once—a leggy giraffe that matched my new sky blue vinyl car coat. When he handed me the little animal and grinned at me as he bent over the fence, I noticed his breath, at ten o'clock on a Wednesday morning, smelling the way my daddy's did late on a Saturday night after poker. Back in class, I put the giraffe on Rose's desk. It blew off when I opened Dr. Seuss, and she did not even watch it fall, much less try to pick it up. I popped him, one leg at a time, on the way home.

That February, it got real cold. Snowed a few inches, which qualifies as severe weather in Alabama where we had neither snowplows, snowsuits, snow tires, nor insulated water pipes, so they closed up school for a couple of days. When the snow turned to mud and slush, we trudged back in. Mrs. Harden, who lived somewhere way out in Romulus, couldn't make it, the roads were so bad. We had a substitute and nobody had thought to explain to her about Rose.

I knew something had happened at Rose's house during that storm from the moment she came in. For one thing, she kept staring out the window at her house, tears rolling down her cheeks. For another, her blouse was dirty with drops of something brown dried on front. She wouldn't sit down, just shook the substitute's hand off her arm when she tried to guide her to her desk. I tried to tell the substitute how it wouldn't do any good to touch Rose or talk to her when we heard the siren coming at us down University Boulevard.

Kids jumped up and ran to the window where Rose stood with the substitute and me. The police and the ambulance pulled up in front of Rose's house, and the men in uniforms stayed inside a long time, then they came back out, talking into little walkie-talkies and wheeling something out covered up on a table. They took away the balloon man with his hands cuffed behind his back. Mrs. Hamner, our principal, came in and led Rose away.

My parents and my grandparents and my aunts all whispered around the dinner table that night while my brother and I sat in front of the television doing our homework and straining to hear. We did not succeed. The only thing I could hear was Aunt Mike whispering, "That poor woman! That poor, poor woman," over and over, and Connie Lee adding, "And her poor baby!" then my mother asking something that sounded to me like "How can a child that age *something unintelligible* and what the hell does half-dead and half-raked mean?" I pictured those broken and rusted tools in Rose's backyard, and wondered if her daddy had hurt her with one of them.

Rose did not come to school the next morning, or the next. As a matter of fact, I never saw Rose again except once in a dream I had. In it, she flew over in a hot air balloon, laughing and waving down at me.

The following Monday, Mrs. Harden returned. Rose's desk was gone. There had been some problems at Rose's house, she explained to us, some very sad problems. Rose would attend a new school from now on, a school where there were other little girls like her. She did not say Bryce's, didn't have to.

Those days, Alabama children prayed in schools. When she saw how puzzled and scared some of us were, how Nonie Myers and I had started to cry, Mrs. Harden asked us to bow our heads and close our eyes and fold our hands on our desktops.

Our teacher prayed out loud for Rose, said a prayer for the little girls who could not play and read and sing and color like us. The Lord, she said, had, in His wisdom, made some of His children different, quiet in ways that we could not understand. Sometimes these differences made it hard for them to learn and make friends. Amen.

We squinted a little when we opened our eyes in the harsh fluorescent light. "Why didn't Rose just . . . ?" Kirby started, but Mrs. Harden hushed him up. It was not our place, she explained, to question the Lord's ways. Clutching in my hand six sticky blue balloons I had found in my desk on Rose's last day, I realized how wrong even the nicest teacher could be.

Some people hurt girls in the name of the Lord.

Once I started working at Bryce's, I tried to spend equal time on all the wards, but of course I developed my favorites—Forensics and Adolescents. The former because lots of them weren't really crazy but had lawyers who managed to get them certified rather than incarcerated. A couple of fine spades players lurked on Forensics, and I got good at the odd version of the game they played, with the big and little joker being the high trumps and the deuce of spades being higher than the ace. Other than that, we played like everybody else. Some days we'd get word that a sorority tour had arrived to view the unfortunate. Residents tried to outdo each other acting nuts. Otis would put down his *Psychology Today,* run to his room, and sit spraddle-legged in front of the door with two Dixie cups stuck upside down in his afro and a rolled-up dishtowel beefing up his crotch. Aaron liked to squat in a ward corner, drooling with his hair backcombed into a rat's nest. And Parnell stared out the window, jumping up and down and screaming, "My mother's coming to see me! My mother's coming to see me! My mother's coming to see me and I'm gonna strangle that bitch when she gets here!" After the poor visitors left, questioning their altruistic dreams of careers in mental health, Otis picked up his magazine, Aaron went back to watching *As the World Turns,* and Parnell sat down across from me and bid six books I knew he probably could not pull. Manics always overbid. We'd finish our game.

On the Adolescent Unit at Bryce, kids that could would sing and laugh and fight, and the ones that couldn't would rock or spell back what you said to them (yes, we had a couple of Rain Men) or amaze you with their delusions and antics. You always had a sense of hope for them, because they were young, their teeth not yet stained with chewing tobacco, their tongues not thickened with medication. We spent our days tie-dying tee-shirts, making and flying kites, learning a dance called the Slide, and drinking and pouring one another Kool-Aid. When I worked there, Adolescents was still on the second floor of one of the old wards—such a light, airy space. A lower-security ward, since most of the patients had no desire to go back to whatever nightmare they'd come from. Once in a while a couple of the boys might climb the fence to attend a Lynnard Skynnard concert or something. They'd show up again soon as they could hitchhike back from Birmingham, though. The tee-shirt and the adventure made giving up a week's worth of grounds privileges worthwhile.

On my first day I was issued two iron keys—one for the front door and one for the ward—each several inches long and almost big around as a ballpoint pen. Every morning I'd check them out from a glass-front cabinet behind the security desk where they hung from a hook with my name on it, and every evening I'd sign them back in. I found them beautiful, and kept them tied together with a green grosgrain ribbon. I wore clothing with pockets deep enough to accommodate them and a pack of Newports (Bryce's currency) and a lighter. After a few days, I could feel without looking or thinking just the angle at which to insert the key, how to anticipate the depth of the lock without overshooting the hundred-year-old mechanism, how you had to hold it straight just so with the same amount of space around the key on each side of the hole to hear the bolt slide. Holding keys and cigarettes guaranteed the lowliest worker a certain degree of respect.

I thought Mary (pronounce it MAY-ree like country people do) was a boy first time I saw her because of the extreme crew cut (and I mean crew)—a colorless stubble barely nubbing up through a translucent scalp—and the gaunt figure, all elbows with no extra flesh anywhere. One of those undernourished boys you might see and think pellagra ran in his family. I changed my mind fast watching the way she had turned in on herself. She didn't cuss at you or spit, did not throw fits or tantrums or chairs or set stuff afire. And she did not smoke or dip snuff, which really made her stand out from the boys who had bludgeoned their stepfathers or the adolescent child molesters who bragged about loving up on four-year-old boys, laughing like they'd gotten caught stealing a pack of Juicy Fruit gum. All Mary did was walk.

The girl would powerwalk twenty years before anyone called it that. Big frantic strides, back and forth the length of the ward with her shoulder skimming the wall. Tilting her head, she would cradle her chin in her right palm with her jaw clenched down so hard that little white skin-puckers popped up around her lips. She kept her green eyes squinted to slits, and once in a while her lips would move and she'd shake her head like she was trying to fling off a bug that had landed in hair she no longer had. You couldn't make out what she was saying. You'd just almost hear syllables she'd whisperspit out of her mouth like something that tasted bad. She wouldn't let you close. Soon as you got your stride caught up good to hers, she'd be gone in some other direction, evading your ears but snatching your curiosity up for the ride.

She wore a secondhand black tee-shirt advertising a Gadsden car dealership, and a pair of baggy jeans that had been cut off—not the way young girls made shorts, but just above where the knees would have been worn through. The hair on her arms and legs was stubble, too—minute colorless spikes sticking up out of skin the color of piecrust dough. You'd notice this more than you'd think because of the sunlight on the ward. The dropped ceilings were sixteen feet high in the old building, and morning light would shoot through the honeycomb of wire octagons embedded in the glass bright enough to make you squint, too. Mary'd squint at whatever she was seeing and you'd squint at her and wonder, and the thousand tiny bristles made the outlines of her arms and her legs and her head jitter like electricity in cartoons, catching light and glinting with her motion.

I started walking, too, but in the opposite direction, every day while the nurse and the aides watched *Secret Storm*—walking not with her, but so we'd cross in opposite directions like shoppers passing on a downtown sidewalk. Finally one day she got used to me walking enough that she slipped up and let me overhear what she muttered. "I don't believe in none of it. I don't believe in none of it," she swore in disgust. "Not in none of it."

Religion undid Mary. I have seen religion in some right quirky manifestations and believe me, honey, speaking in tongues ain't jack. One girl down the road had a momma who told her Santa was Satan with two letters reversed and would slide down the chimney and eat her alive if she didn't stop sassing. Claud Clarke's aunt Etoile held his head in a hot oven to show him what the fires of Hell would feel like if he ever partook of alcoholic beverages the way his daddy did. And once when I was thirteen I went with my lockermate to a church where a man drank a gas tank additive out of a Dixie cup to prove his faith in a God he thought might strike him dead before dinnertime if he didn't. I guess that's why I found the story in Mary's chart believable.

She came from somewhere up in north Alabama where the three main sources of income were stripping down and reselling hot cars, climbing over fences to steal chickens from a poultry-processing plant, and painting serpents on the sides of churches. Her momma had made her drop out of school young because her teacher did not fear the Lord the way she ought to. She married Mary off to the preacher. She'd run home a few times that first month, but they kept carrying her back, apologizing and begging the clergyman's patience on account of her age, because after all, she only had fourteen years to his fifty-seven. I guess she tried to settle in and be a wife the way she ought to, only she did not know how yet. Not much to speak of in the cooking and conjugal duty departments.

Turns out he's the one who didn't believe in none of it. After he figured he had her broken of running off, he took her into Northport one day and almost got himself arrested when he came out of the bank and saw her through the drugstore window, squirting a perfume sample on her hair and her wrist, preening and sniffing at herself like a biblical harlot. The preacher yanked her out by her elbow and shoved her into his truck.

He figured there was nothing to do to mend her whorish ways but take Mary home and shave her, and that's what he did—took the girl out to their shack about seventeen miles from everywhere and dry-stripped every hair off her body with his own well-used straight razor. Sometime after nightfall, she finally worked her wrists out of the rope in the backyard where he'd left her hung up. That's when Mary took her first fast walk.

In spite of the ankle she sprained falling, she made it to the house of a neighbor of another faith while her own spouse was off saving souls at a revival in the next county. Mr. Larkin and his wife were in the living room down on their knees trying to rig the antenna from a DeSoto station wagon to their TV set so they could see *Laugh-In* better when they heard Mary knocking. Lord knows what they thought when they found her at their door a week before Thanksgiving, naked as a new-hatched jaybird and nicked bloody eyebrow to kneecap, the Reverend not having been blessed with a steady razor hand. Authorities were notified. I believe there was some litigating around the incident and the congregation was left without spiritual guidance for several months. After that, it seemed like Mary simply could not stop walking, limping a little on account of her bad ankle, so her people packed her off to Bryce's.

Mary and I passed like that on the ward several times a day, her sliding along the plaster wall and me trying to look uninterested. After a few weeks of that, she got to where she'd acknowledge my presence by sometimes walking around me instead of making me step around her. One day, I decided to make my move. I kept stepping in front of her. Every time she'd move left, I'd move right, like those two unacquainted shoppers were trying to pass and not succeeding. I wouldn't make eye contact, but I saw her start grinning a little on the left side of her face before she caught herself and shook the smile away. She scrunched her eyes up and hissed, "I don't believe in none of it!" And I looked right back and said, "Well, Mary, I do. I believe in this." I reached in my pocket and pulled out the Newports. I put two in my mouth and lit both, the way high school boys do when they're trying to act like movie stars the morning after.

She took it when I offered, and I changed direction. That was our first time walking together. We never spoke much, although once she did whisper, "I like walking. It's fun."

I wish I could tell you it was her big breakthrough, her Helen-at-the-water-pump moment, only I'd be lying. We never made much more progress than these walking and smoking sessions. I'd just get in step with her and pull out two and light them up. One day I did manage to half-drag and half-bait her onto the Adolescent Unit bus and take her on a skating trip with sixteen other residents. Once we got to the rink, Bob and I laced her into a pair of skates and hauled her out onto the floor.

I would not go so far as to say Mary could skate, but she did pretty much what she did back on the ward. She had better balance than you'd expect. After a few scoots of her bad foot, she glided from leg to leg, right along the wall, muttering to herself to the rhythm of the wheels about her convictions. Bob and I let her be, keeping closer watch on boys likely to cause trouble when their worlds collided with those of the unincarcerated.

One of these boys was Kyley Reese, the gorgeous thirteen-year-old offspring of a black jazz sax man. Every time he'd go for a home visit, Kyley's Polynesian momma would send him back with five bottles of sunscreen and a note instructing us to slather him up good any time he went outside. Kyley started trying to get some town girl to skate double with him to "Never Can Say Goodbye," and got to being a little too insistent. She lit out and Kyley lit out after her and I lit out after him and grabbed his shirt like my mother had raised a fool. He spun around on me, teeth bared and fists balled up, rared back to swing, when the skate on Mary Buford's good foot caught him right upside his head. She did not say a word to him or to me, just came at him dead-on hard as she could like a kick-boxer on wheels. She did not knock Kyley cold, but he hit hardwood sputtering, and later took thirteen stitches on his forehead.

Bob told me that evening what scared him most was the way Mary turned and gave three pushes with the foot that made contact and slid right back along that wall like nothing had happened, leaving a single little roller-track of blood. I could not argue. What scared me more, though, was the look in her eye. Bob did not see it and I never told him or anyone else. Confidentiality and all, but I guess I can tell now. It's been almost thirty years.

I have seen some looks in my life that I would describe as rage and I have witnessed one or two you might call cold-blooded, but what I saw in Mary's face that day beat both. It was like the way she might look at the devil if she saw him on the road—a glare to tell him that she not only recognized him for who and what he was, but that she was ready and willing to extract retribution for every wrong he'd done. And I swear to you, she smiled when wheel hit temple.

I gave notice shortly after. In this world, I know things like what happened to Mary happen every day, but it just hurts too much when you see them up close in that harsh ward light. When I turned in my keys to the charge nurse, I gave her two cartons of Newports. "You give these to Mary Buford," I told her. I just hope Mary was able to get them lit. Mary wasn't the type they let handle fire, but maybe she let somebody else get close enough.

Remember the Little Match Girl? Andersen, but it read more like Grimm. First time I heard it my ballet teacher read it to us in preparation for a recital piece she'd choreographed. I cried so hard my mother had to take off work to come and get me. My revulsion may have been a premonition.

Long story short, her daddy ran her out of the house to sell matches on Christmas Eve. Nobody's buying. Pitiful-looking wisp draped in rags. People ran from her, probably, turned to avoid making eye contact like we do today when people stand on the median advertising their desire to work for food. Lacking the ability to entice customers, Match Girl looked pretty much doomed to freeze. Head home and her father would whup her for empty pockets. Lighting just a match or two might warm up her fingers. And the strike of each match hissed up a vision.

First match showed her a warm wood stove so real she could see her reflection in the polished brass feet. She basked for a minute, thawed till the match burnt out. Second match sat her right down in front of a fancy dinner, roasted goose I believe it was. Before she got a good mouthful, damned match blistered her finger. No more supper, Match Girl.

Next match brought her a Christmas tree, lit up bright with candles casting shadows on a hundred presents underneath, all of them for her. Turned out, of course, her only gift was the burnt-out match. I believe it was her dead grandmother ended up taking her to Heaven. Constable found her next morning, a frozen little corpse with three burnt matches and a handful of blisters.

They don't make fairy tales like they used to. Lots of the old ones fell from favor, too grim for today's little play-date children. Believe me, though; working in mental health, I saw plenty of places where that match girl could make herself right at home.

Little girl babies come into this world with nothing to get them by except their own ability to charm. That failing, things turn ugly fast, especially when her parents are ignorant and scared, or just plain mean, or when the child is born into a particularly uncharmable family.

Geneva arrived at Chestnut Branch Children's Center nine months to the day after my new-employee orientation. Mr. Alden taught us how the point system worked, showed us safe restraint techniques for kids who were trying to hurt themselves or other kids or us. My reflexes weren't shabby, and I could dodge a flung folding chair as well as the next counselor. After Bryce's, the University of Alabama's model program felt like Shangri-La. Only ten kids on each residential unit at a time, and three staff members for each unit. Homelike atmosphere. Cable TV. And when the age range is seven to eleven you can actually hope that some of your charges might get better, have decent lives. Most did.

Three beautiful buildings nestled on ten wooded acres; bird feeders and binoculars; money to take the children out to eat and to the movies and to go swimming. You could take pride in what you did. Some parents showed up for weekly visits with a soft-spoken psychologist and learned behavioral techniques to handle tough disciplinary problems in effective and nonabusive ways. A few kids who did not have parents even got adopted. One boy, Sonny, sent us a Valentine photograph of him a year later, bat in hand, grinning in his Little League uniform.

One catch, though. Kids had to be in big trouble to get to Chestnut Branch on state money. A child's behavior had to be truly outrageous for the school system to be willing to foot the bill. For boys, we were usually talking violence. A few of our boys had killed other children. We did not get that many girls, and the ones who came had to be turned in on themselves badly enough to scare you.

Geneva was tiny for ten years. Her face had tight lines around her lips and the smartest little foxlike eyes. Never missed a trick. A headful of brown curls that did everything but what they were supposed to. She walked with a slight limp, but you had to watch close to see it. Her left hand trembled a little when she ate or wrote. I offered her a seat by the television, but all she wanted to do was sweep that first evening. We let her. When I took the broom and put my hand on her shoulder an hour before bedtime, she threw her arms around me and began to sob.

I took her into the kitchen to get her a sandwich since she had missed supper. Our selection of canned soft drinks dazzled her for a moment before she went for the Dr Pepper. It worked on her like a cocktail. We sat in the kitchen while she ate a PB and J and handful of Oreos. She was a good reader, she told me. She liked cats a lot. Her favorite color was yellow or rainbow. As Geneva spoke, suddenly confident, an uneasiness came over me. I tried to shrug it off, but it stuck.

After being quiet in their beds for five minutes, each child got a goodnight visit with a counselor. I sat on the side of the bed and reminded them of something good they had done during the day, something sweet or funny, hoping to help them have happy dreams. I never have felt particularly maternal or desired a child of my own. I just figured most of these kids had precious little sweet in their lives and a bit of special wouldn't hurt them. A kiss on the forehead, a song, or a little poem. When I put Geneva to bed, I did the rhyme that became hers, touching her face with my fingertip, chanting:

> Here's where the cat sits.
> Here's where he jumps.
> Eye-winker,
> Tom Tinker,
> Nose-dropper,
> Mouth-eater,
> Chin-chopper,
> Gotcha, gotcha, gotcha, gotcha, gotcha!

She laughed when I finished the chin tickle, and closed her eyes, covers tucked up to her chin. As I was leaving, she asked me quietly, "Can you please get me some lotion for my foot?" I asked her what was wrong with it. She sat up and pulled back the covers.

I tried not to recoil when I saw the red shiny puckers of the burn scars. Bad ones, the kind you get from grafts, patterned and shiny like crocodile skin but with raised white ridges. "It itches me sometimes," she said.

I brought in a bottle of lotion from the office. Resting her little foot on my thigh, I gingerly began massaging in the lotion, barely touching the surface of her skin. "Does it hurt?"

"Not anymore. Just itches." She studied my face in the shadowlight from the open door, and I was careful not to let her see me react.

Face hot, I hurried to the office when the lotion was absorbed and pulled her file. According to her face sheet, the scars on Geneva's foot were the result of an attempt by her parents to end her seizures. They decided, after trying God-knows-what other methods, that this wasn't no seizure. They could not afford seizures. Nothing but another one of her goddamn tantrums. Momma put the water on to boil in a soup pot. Even though the seizure was over by the time it bubbled up high, her daddy stuck her left foot in it, and held it there till she stopped screaming. The next day at school, her teacher asked about the limp. Evidently some skin came off with her sock. The authorities got involved.

Every day I pushed my discomfort with Geneva aside. I put her to bed at night. This became our ritual—Here's where the cat sits. Tickle and a kiss and a foot massage. What she wanted, wronged child that she was, was not so much emollient as unflinching witness. Pain in the spotlight and me there with her, facing it, holding it, touching it with tenderness. I never asked myself or her how she survived it. Tough smart kid. I did wonder how anyone human could hold the miracle of a little girl's foot and think to do it harm.

Geneva sat coloring a picture of a wolf one day when suddenly her eyes cut sharp to the right, looking at me and past me, not blinking. At the same time, her chin dropped down and popped out of joint like it had dropped its hinge. Her lower back teeth ground against her upper front ones so hard I thought her jaw would crack, and she rocked and grinned so wide it looked as if her face might split. She bared those teeth and growled gut rhythms from her throat.

No convulsions. The seizure lasted three, maybe four minutes. Then she drank her entire Dr Pepper without lowering the bottle and sank down with her head on the table. I called Ricky and we carried her to her bed. The nurse came and pronounced her fine, said she'd sleep for a while, then probably be very hungry when she awoke. She instructed us to explain to Geneva when she awoke that she'd had a little seizure. We should feed her a normal supper.

Doctors thought her seizures the result of some sort of head injury in infancy. Geneva took medication for them, and the meds were frequently changed. Some made her sleepy. One made her salivate excessively. Some simply did not work. She'd seem to benefit for a while, then build up a resistance to the medicine's efficacy, as if the seizure wanted so much to happen that it would find its way out. Seeing Geneva's seizure, I understood how people can believe in possession. She snarled and tensed every muscle, looking at me like she'd starved all her life and I was all she could eat.

It was her seizures that freed her from her torturers and got her to Chestnut Branch. She did not act out in any way when she first came. Her former teachers had described her as smart, eager to please, always volunteering for classroom chores. She especially liked to sweep the steps down to the playground. There was just something about her, though, something that was not right, that made people want to get as far away from her as they could.

Long as she got her medication, she did fine. She reminded her teacher when one o'clock came, washed her pills down with Dr Pepper. In the absence of Dr Pepper, she crunched the pills between her teeth. Seeing one seizure, though, other children would not go near her, and even the student teacher did not like to. After her mother's arrest, Geneva simply had nowhere to go. Her father jumped bail, and no foster home would take her because of her seizure activity.

Unfortunately, Geneva had a talent for mimicry. You know how some people can pick the exact nuance, the turn of head, the subtlety of intonation and accent so that everybody knows exactly whom they are imitating? That was Geneva. And at Chestnut Branch, she had a curiosity shop of extreme behaviors to understudy.

And she learned them all. Excelled. By the end of a few months, Geneva realized that the kids who got the most attention, who had the most power in the group, were the ones whose behavior demanded intervention. Standing in line quietly might earn you an extra hour of television at night, but smear shit on a wall or set off a fire alarm or scream that your teacher was a motherfucking ass-sucker during story hour and you'll garner yourself some real attention. Everything stops and you hold court at the world's center. You roar out your rage and nobody beats you up or boils your appendages. Intoxicating power. Anger becomes art. By the end of a few months, the other kids were all afraid of Geneva. Hell, we all were. It took me and Ricky both to restrain her if she really got going. She'd soaked up each child's worst and spit it back at us, amplified. Staff began to use words like psychotic. Liability. Unadoptable.

After Geneva cut loose and started her reign of terror, I figured out what made us afraid of her, even when she was acting good. When she behaved well, she'd put Shirley Temple to shame, as if she had analyzed what sort of behavior would make her audience see her as angelic. When she wanted to cause you fear or embarrassment, she could hone right in on the thing that would hurt you most. Eerie, the way she ferreted out those parts of your soul you hoped never saw the light of day. When put in time-out by Carl, who worked three jobs to pay child support, she'd laugh in his face and sneer, "What happened to your car, you fat-ass nigger? Re-po man find you again?" When pulled off of a child she'd attacked by Sherry, a counselor private about her sexual preference, she'd wink and leer, growling, "Hey, sweet thing, why don't you come see me after lights out? I'll show you a real hot time." And it made you afraid when you had to intervene, terrified that she would pounce on whatever weakness you had and lay it out for the world to view.

Most kids had somewhere to go that Christmas, even the killers. Home for a day visit, sometimes supervised by a social worker. A charitable foster family, a grandmother's house. Not Geneva. Nowhere at Christmas or any other time. Our social worker asked me if I would take one hundred dollars of state money, supplemented by thirty dollars from our activities fund, to buy her some gifts. My mother kicked in a little more, and a few of the other counselors contributed. By the time I was done, I had collected around two hundred dollars, which was a pretty healthy Christmas fund for a homeless child in the 1970s. Before I knew it, damned if I hadn't volunteered to take her home with me for three days, including Christmas.

I meant well. I reckon I just was not thinking. Me a college student, not prepared to take care of any child, much less one like Geneva. Home a tiny upstairs apartment in a Victorian house, shared with a geriatric cat. I practically lived on grits and Campbell's soup. No car in a town without public transportation. I rode a bike everywhere I went.

No desire to be anyone's mother, either. What I did have, and what made me good at my job at Chestnut Branch, was a good memory of how I wanted to be treated when I was a child. And in spite of our own brand of dysfunction, my family usually managed to pull off a pretty good Christmas.

When Otis delivered Geneva to my home on the twenty-third, her hair was still damp at the part where she had wet it to try to comb it smooth. She stepped into my living room clutching a grocery bag of her few belongings. I set about making her at home, showing her where she was to sleep, the drawer I had cleared for her clothes. She bent to sniff the yellow scentless grocery-store chrysanthemums I had arranged on her night table, turned to me and said, "Thank you, Melissa."

I put her to greasing the pan and measuring while I read her the instructions on a box of Pillsbury brownie mix. We walked down to the corner to buy Popsicles. I did with her the things I loved as a child, hoping she would love them too.

And sometimes during those days, I caught her looking at me with something close to pity or compassion in her face. She recognized what I was doing, what we were both doing. We were acting. She was pretending to be a whole child, one who had been allowed to be sweet and happy. I was pretending to be a loving adult, a mother of sorts, who lived to nurture and guard the girl in her care. I sat down on the sofa and pulled her onto my lap and began to rock. Wordlessly, we agreed to continue the charade.

I had already put the lights on my Christmas tree so Geneva would not hear me cuss. I had saved the fun part, the tinsel and ornaments for her. That night, I built a little fire in the tiny coal grate that would never have passed inspection, and read her "The Night Before Christmas." We set out milk and a brownie for a saint neither of us believed in. When she slept, I put her gifts, each tied up with a yellow bow, under our tree.

She opened them early that morning, with appropriate squeals and expressions of joy. Poor girl had nothing. I had bought her a pretty dress. A school outfit, a pair of good jeans, and a pair of sneakers. The requisite socks and underwear. A pair of Mary Janes. A nightgown imprinted with dancing cats. I had filled a Kmart cart with toys — a paint set, a book of fairy tales, a fluffy stuffed cat to cuddle at night. A couple of card games. Maybe someone would play. Bubble bath. A book of jokes. A pretend make-up set. A magic kit. A giant pump bottle of Jergen's lotion.

My mother picked us up and took us to her house for Christmas dinner. My warning about the chaos Geneva was capable of causing proved unnecessary. She sat up straight in the new dress, napkin on lap, and politely asked for seconds on stuffing, washing it down with Dr Pepper. Before we left, we watched *Miracle on 34th Street* on my mother's big television. She gave my mother a goodbye, as well as a foil-wrapped brownie she had thought to bring without my knowledge.

This is not one of those "all she needed was a little love" stories. I don't kid myself, and don't you. People way better prepared than I was have found it impossible to deal with the problems a child that bruised can have. A three-day Christmas visit is not day-to-day life, with the added stress of school, work, childcare, and the real world.

Ricky gave us a ride back to the center later on Christmas Day. I sat in the back seat with Geneva, ready to restrain her if I had to, afraid she might pitch a fit. She did not. She sat next to me, silent, looking out the window.

When we got back, she put her new toys and clothes away, took off her new shoes. The children who had only temporary Christmas arrangements came trickling back in. We suspended the usual rules. Everyone stayed up late and we ordered pizza for dinner.

When I put Geneva to bed, I told her how much I had enjoyed her visit, thanked her for sharing Christmas with me. As I began rubbing the lotion into her little foot, I told her we could make a ritual of it if she liked, that we could do it again the coming year. When I tried to do "Here's where the cat sits," she turned away. I kissed the curls that fell across her forehead, asked her if she wanted anything before she went to bed. She told me she had a headache.

I got her two children's aspirins and a Dr Pepper. When I brought them, I found her sobbing, not like a little girl, but the way a heartbroken woman sobs, deep in her chest, racking. I held her crooning and rocking until she quietened a little.

She took the aspirin with shaky hands, swallowed. Took a sip. "You sure do love Dr Pepper." I smiled weakly.

"I get it from my mother. She used to give me a sip of hers when I quit crying."

I wish I could tell you her behavior improved after this, that our sweet Christmas together was healing in deep and abiding ways, but I'd be lying. Soon, Geneva picked up her old antics and invented some new ones. She became more disruptive, attacked one boy with a screwdriver. That year, a friend told me about another job. Cushy, better pay, no chairs flying at my head.

Chestnut Branch. Hardest job I ever left. I kept waiting till this child or that one got through the program, got set down safe somewhere. Finally I realized there would always be that child. I made my speech to the children I left, said my goodbyes to the staff, and walked.

I did not forget my promise to Geneva. A few weeks before Christmas the following year, I called to make sure she had a place to spend the holiday. Mr. Alden, the director, explained that she had hurt a child, thrown a glass of Dr Pepper against a wall and cut his head badly. They'd put her on a locked ward at Bryce's.

Children did not get rhymes and kisses at bedtime out at Bryce's when I worked there. I tell myself that maybe they did by the time Geneva moved in. If she still lives there and if she remembers me in the moments when the lights are out before she sleeps, I know she will forgive me for not being who she wanted me to be. I hope she knows that when she was ten years old she was my little girl on

Christmas Eve, and that she came as close to charming me as any child could. And I hope the vision of that Christmas left no scar if it ever burned out.

I knew these girls so long ago, but I know some things, thanks to them, that help me still. In the second grade, I learned not to flinch in the face of ugliness. I can still bid a respectable spades hand. And I know how holy it can feel to put a child peacefully to bed. Years after working in mental health, I went back to graduate school and became an archivist. With all those face sheets and critical-incident reports, handmade Valentines and refrigerator pictures, I've really been one most of my life anyway.

I have kept the archives of the girls turned in, their ephemera: blue balloons, roller skates, cigarette butts, and lotion bottles. Silenced by their youth or their poverty, they don't leave letters. If they get hurt enough to be swept into the mental health system, laws passed to protect their privacy ensure their invisibility over time.

In her poem "Kathe Kollwitz," Muriel Rukeyser wrote, "What would happen if one woman told the truth about her life? The world would split open." In the part of Alabama where I come from, lots of girls and women have histories that disturb. The earth has not split yet, and if what those girls suffered has not split it, Alabama will probably remain intact. Stories do not move earth, and to tell you the truth, they do not seem to move families, schools, state governments, or God to do much better by the precious girls in their care.

But each girl's tale has its own power, its own parable to ponder. I've heard a slew of such tales over the years. These stuck with me, shamed me, made me wonder how I could have done better.

Come up close like that and getting a good night's sleep becomes impossible if you don't bear witness. You don't think about them all the time, but one day, a carny offers you a balloon dachshund at the state fair or a homeless woman asks you for a light, and it hits you hard: those girls still hang onto your hem and they always will. While their stories may not split the earth, there's this place I know right across the highway from where I grew up where those girls all came together, and every fall a cloud catches on fire and crashes right down. I can barely stand to look, it burns so bright. So close to the river, and almost in my own front yard.

sightline books . . . .
The Iowa Series in Literary Nonfiction